L. Jean Watson
Endowed
Fund

He's Making You Crazy

KRISTEN DOUTE

with MICHELE ALEXANDER

CHICAGO
REVIEW
PRESS

Copyright © 2020 by Kristen Doute and Michele Alexander
All rights reserved
Published by Chicago Review Press Incorporated
814 North Franklin Street
Chicago, Illinois 60610
ISBN 978-1-64160-379-9

Library of Congress LCCN: 2020932405

Interior design: Sarah Olson

Printed in the United States of America
5 4 3 2 1

To the guys that made me crazy.
And to my mom, for being a badass and undercover crazy.

Contents

PART THREE: *Kamikaze Kristen*

PART FOUR: *Kickin' It Single*

PART FIVE: *Kumbaya, Bitches*

INTRODUCTION

The Dreaded C-Word

IF THERE'S ONE THING I know, it's crazy. A *lot* of people have called me crazy. Crazy Kristen! For a while there, it was practically my name. Women all over the world get called crazy every day. But we weren't born crazy—we were *made* crazy. It's true, and I have plenty of stories to prove it. My turbulent dating history has brought me an abundance of peaks and valleys, but I didn't get there on my own. Crazy is a two-person job.

We start out as innocent, glowing little girls, full of sugar and spice and everything nice. Boys are "gross" because they're just our buddies, until one day they're not so gross anymore, and we're doodling hearts in our notebooks, adding their last name to ours. We always think the first guy we date is the one we're going to marry. Hell, we think *every* guy we date is the one we're going to marry! It just doesn't ever end up that way, and each new disappointment drives you a little bit crazier.

Some guys—most every guy I've had the pleasure of dating—were masters of manipulation. They would gaslight me and play champion jujitsu-level mind games. They could instantaneously make me feel insecure, second-guess myself, and provoke me to (severely) overreact. This only made me feel needier, more co-dependent, more emotional, and yes, even *crazy*.

You may not think you need or even want any advice on relationships from someone like me, but trust me: with my long history of bad decisions, bad breakups, and the occasional melt-down in the wake of those breakups, you will definitely at least learn from my mistakes what *not* to do.

Possibly contrary to popular belief, I take full responsibility for my life. I'm here to poke a little fun at myself and, more important, at all these guys who were dismissive of my feelings, downplayed everything they had ever done, made me feel ridic-ulous for being upset, and accused me of being too dramatic. We've all been through it, and some of my stories are definitely yours too.

We're all familiar with the nature-versus-nurture debate from high school, but let me break it down for you when it comes to relationships between men and women:

NATURE: *Maybe* we, as women, can be a bit erratic, a bit overly analytical, a bit irrational.

NURTURE: *He* is *making* us crazy. The lies, the late nights, the laziness, the lies—did I already say the lies? And it's not just one "He"; it's a lot of them, over years and years. The glorification of being in the perfect relationship makes us crazy. The romanticization of being with the perfect guy makes us crazy. And the impossibility of both makes us crazier.

It's nurture that really does the trick.

Ladies, think about your first crush. It probably didn't end well, unless you're married to him now, in which case: congratu-*fucking*-lations. Please gift this glorious read to all of your single friends. You are a unicorn.

Guys, this book is also for you. I'm not here to go psycho because you call me crazy. I'm here to *own* my crazy—and to gently explain to you why it's mostly your fault. You might not like taking the heat for what you've done, but in the end . . . can you blame us?

Deep down, you love crazy bitches.

PART ONE

Killing My Innocence

A View from the Top

LET'S START HERE: I was born tall.

I think I was at full-grown, five-foot-nine, Amazonian stature at the age of thirteen. I wasn't insecure about it; I was a self-confident young lady, still raising my hand in class assertively. You see, in middle school the battle of the sexes is extremely lop-sided: Girls run the world. Boys are scared of us. They are just beginning to like us, and they don't know what to do about it. At that age, for a brief moment, we hold all the cards; just a tiny hint of boobs gives us major power.

This dynamic changes fairly quickly as we go through life, facing challenges, breakups, assholes, and losers, and suddenly that untouched self-esteem is out the window. I wish I had known then what I know now, and held on to that inconceivable feeling of power for a little while longer. Unfortunately power doesn't always come with wisdom.

I was in Ms. Shelton's language arts class when I heard that
the most popular girl in our grade had just had her first kiss
during Mr. Jefferson's PE class. I now had a mission: it was time
for *my* first kiss. I was thirteen—a *teenager!*—and I was ready.

He was the most popular guy in our class and he was the chosen one, whether he liked it or not. He was short, much shorter
than me—I'm talking tiny, adorable little pip-squeak short. I
didn't care, dammit. This Mr. Petite was going to be *mine* by the
end of the school day. I enlisted my BFF to make the rounds with
me past his locker between classes. I waited until the bell rang
and slipped a note in his locker, sealed with a Lip Smacker–fla-
vored kiss.

"Do you want to be my first
kiss? Check YES or YES." I was
confident it would be yes. "See
you after school. Be there or be
square."

The last bell finally rang, and
word had spread that Mr. Petite
and I had a date with destiny at
his locker at exactly 3:15. My
friends and I gathered in the
bathroom one last time for a quick pep talk and a zhuzh of the
hair. The walk to Mr. Petite's locker was like a slow-mo, syn-
chronized scene from any '90s rom-com. My confidence was pal-
pable. We turned the corner and there he was, looking fly, like
a young Vince Vaughn in *Swingers*. If he'd been old enough to
drink, he'd have had a vodka martini in his hand—shaken, not
stirred.

Once we were in striking distance of each other, it became obvious that this kiss wasn't going to happen, at least not without a little bit of . . . well, a boost.

Before we could even think of the consequences, my best friend scooped him up from his waist and lifted him toward me. It was awkward, like all first kisses should be. His rock-hard gelled crooner hairdo thumped my forehead first before we realized we had to tilt our heads so as not to smash our faces together. You would think kissing would be an instinctual activity learned through osmosis, but it's not. Kissing takes practice. (If you don't think it does, then you are doing it wrong.) The whole incident lasted a cool five seconds before my BFF released Mr. Petite down to his normal location in the world.

And, just like that, it was over. I had survived my first kiss.

I woke up the next day, feeling . . . pretty much the same. Nothing had changed for me. A kiss *was* just a kiss. Yet once I got to school, the air felt different. Something was going on.

Between the whispers in the hallway and the notes being passed around, I figured out that Mr. Petite had spread a rumor that we went to second base. We didn't, but everyone believed him. Apparently our height difference humiliated him to the point that he sought his revenge in the most childish way. His lies ruined my reputation at school, and I was immediately labeled a slut. I'd started the year super confident and unashamed of my feelings, and this betrayal was the first of many that chipped away at my belief in myself.

I learned quickly that guys will go for the jugular. If you bruise their ego, they're coming after you hard—and I guess in the seventh grade, the jugular was my tits.

It didn't ruin me; I still knew my worth. But I filed this lesson away in my back pocket.

Family Affair

SORRY IN ADVANCE if you are hearing this for the first time, but if you have a hot brother, chances are you have a *lot* of friends who are using you to get to him.

Getting close to the family is stalker-in-training 101. Daily proximity to the man you love gives you the opportunity to gather intel on the regular, which is a major leg up on the competition.

To be clear, this didn't start out as a user situation. I genuinely liked his sister! But her brother quickly became the main attraction, and he gave me just enough attention to keep me on the hamster wheel. Meanwhile, not only was I becoming best friends with his sister, his parents were in love with me too. I could do no wrong. They needed dishes washed? I was there. Laundry? I'll show you how many Tommy Hilfiger briefs I can fold in an hour. Movie nights? I made the popcorn.

He'd hang out with me *-ish*, but I had some real work to do. He still thought of me as his little sister's friend, even though he and I were the same age.

I needed to make him think of me as the only viable match, his match made in heaven. I needed to reinvent myself in his eyes.

REINVENTION TACTIC 1: *Be More Mature*

Act older and wiser than you are, and always try to play it cool. Read a book, watch the news, and catch *SportsCenter* once in a while. No more Saturday morning cartoons.

After spending the day reading the first few chapters of *Harry Potter* and catching *60 Minutes* between *7th Heaven* commercials, I sat next to him on the couch, so close that I could smell his deodorant.

I changed the channel to ESPN and asked him if he thought the Pistons were going to win the World Series. He laughed! I laughed! I didn't know why we were laughing, but I didn't really care. We. Were. Laughing. Together!

REINVENTION TACTIC 2: *No More Pajamas*

You can't just wake up after your sleepover with his sister and mosey straight down to the kitchen for breakfast with his family anymore. You have to pull it together if you want him to see you in a different light. This is a perfect opportunity to wear cute short shorts, maybe a sexy T-shirt, and not seem like you're trying too hard. You can't help it, you just woke up like that! (Bonus points if your chosen family has a pool—bikini all day, every day.)

On the first night of my Reinvention Tour, I went to Contempo Casuals and bought a zillion thongs and practiced wearing them. After a few days, I went to his house wearing them high on the sides, and made sure to bend over near him so he could see the "whale tail" from my thong.

REINVENTION TACTIC 3: *Form a Strong Bond*

You need to have your own inside jokes that are just between the two of you. Make up a funny but ah-*dorable* nickname for him—he'll probably make one up for you too. Emphasize what you already have in common.

After several weeks of trying, I found ways to spend time with him alone. The fam would bake cookies and I'd offer to take them to his room. We'd share a joke and I'd giggle and slap him on the arm and tell him to "Stawp it."

I purposely took the chain off my bike and asked him to fix it for me. We sat in the driveway of his house for over twelve minutes total together, alone—chatting, laughing, and *bonding*.

One time he saved a seat for me on the school bus. It was typically reserved for his baseball buddy, but on that day that seat was mine. Normally I sat with his sister, but I couldn't pass up this epic opportunity, so I ditched her. I thought she would understand—until I felt the daggers of her stare coming from the front of the bus.

Whatever. I was swooning. I started calling him My Romeo. Instead of the Capulets and the Montagues, it was only his sister keeping the two of us apart. We were modern-day star-crossed lovers.

REINVENTION TACTIC 4: *Become Super Good at Something He's Good At*

This one is pretty self-explanatory. Unless it's wrestling, you can be just as good as him at anything, and usually better. (Don't tell him you're better; guys can be delicate daffodils.) It gives you another reason to spend more time with him.

My Romeo was addicted to PlayStation, so I practiced playing *Madden NFL* for hours on end, every night and every weekend, learning all of the cheat codes. His special teams were his Achilles's heel, so I knew he would appreciate the code for a better kicker.

"Thanks, BIGFOOT," he said. *A pet name!*

REINVENTION TACTIC 5: *Be Best Friends with His Best Friends*

If his friends see you as an option, he will too.

I grew up in Metro Detroit, and one of the great things about living in Michigan are the basements. The Midwest totally gets down with making their basements the number-one place to hang out for every occasion. I'd say a big percentage of Michigander babies are conceived in Michiganders' basements.

I was finally able to arrange the gathering I'd fantasized about all year. I invited all of his buddies, with me and his sister as the only girls. To keep his sister off my trail, I had masterminded her crushing on his best friend the whole time. That way, when we got dolled up together, no red flags were raised. *Genius*.

We made cupcakes, stocked up on Faygo Red Pop, and had our CD stack full of Boyz II Men, Bon Jovi, and TLC to set the mood. By this point My Romeo and I had dozens of inside jokes. Our eyes would lock for so long sometimes you'd think we were having a staring contest, and I just needed to wait for the right time to suggest a playful game of Spin the Bottle.

If you plan in advance and practice with the right bottle, in the right location, and have all the variables set . . . there's a 99 percent chance you can spin that thing exactly to where and on whom you want it to land. If you try it on linoleum, it just takes a twist of the wrist. Carpet can be a little tricky; the grooves of the yarn might catch the bottle and send it in the wrong direction, so be sure to lift it a little. Glass is fast and hard to control, so try to divert from any glass surface.

I found the best solution for any base: take your time to survey the area like a pro golfer would on a tee. Assess every angle possible. Make sure to clear any loose particles that might alter your precise spin and send your bottle to the wrong person. Lint is a bitch. I was young, and I had plenty of time to waste on such an incredibly important undertaking.

It was a no-brainer that we would end up playing Spin the Bottle, and I knew I was finally going to get my kiss. And, when we finally touched lips, there weren't just sparks, there were full-blown fireworks! (And I could tell he liked it too.)

The following week I had plans to go see the Cranberries at Pine Knob with him and his family. Would we kiss again? Would this be the night he was finally going to ask me to go steady? The forecast was sunny with a chance of L-O-V-E.

When they came to pick me up in the minivan, I couldn't wait to jump in the back into my regular seat next to him. And there *she* was, with her extra-wavy blonde ponytail, holding hands with him. His date. Had I just been disposable to him? Where had she been all this time? I had put in the work—what did *she* do? And she was wearing what I can only describe as the lamest outfit I'd ever seen: a neon skort and knockoff Uggs. Who wears *that* to a Cranberries concert?

When we got to the concert it turned out my designated seat was on the opposite end of his, with five bodies between us. I couldn't even pay attention to the show because I was too busy side-eyeing their PDA. He had his arm around her the entire time. *How could his parents allow this?* When "Dreams" came on they were laughing and flirting, and I was tearing up in misery. I pouted internally the entire show thinking, *Did he have to let it linger?* I was crushed. I had to come to terms with the fact that he just *didn't* look at me the same way he looked at this other girl.

This is the thing about guys. He gave me just enough attention, a glimmer of hope that he and I might actually have a future. It was just a game for him, and I didn't see through it. Instead I wasted my precious time reinventing my *awesome* self for him, which it turns out is something you should never do.

Puppy Love

IT WAS FRESHMAN YEAR of high school and I was in crisis mode. Most of my friends were well past second base, and I wasn't even allowed to date yet. I refused to fall behind.

We had a "Senior/Freshman Day" at the beginning of the year where all the freshman got to choose a senior to escort them to class for the day. I knew walking in day one who my pick would be: it was my cousin's best friend's sister's neighbor on the left side, down by the Kroger grocery store. He was the hottest guy in school, so *of course* I knew exactly who he was!

I had crushed on him for years prior. I was ten when I first noticed him. He raked our leaves, and I wrote him poetry. This was now my chance, as I had one full year where we would be in school together, walking the same halls every single day. I mean, I was fourteen going on fifteen! I was a woman now, right?

I made sure I was the first to the sign-up sheet so I could claim him. (Small victory!) He had to walk me to all of my classes, carry my books for me, *and* sit with me at lunch. That would equal exactly ninety minutes of solo quality time together. Was this our first date? I wanted to be face to face with those dimples, and I *always* got what I wanted. I only needed eighty-nine minutes for him to fall in love with me.

I was a great flirt. He started carrying my books by choice and asking me to skip lunch to go to Taco Bell with him in his pickup truck. Finally, one night after his football game, he put his varsity jacket over my shoulders and asked me to come over and watch a movie. I couldn't believe my mom allowed it. This was the very first time my mom allowed me to ride in a car with a guy. (She knew his parents, so that's why I was given the go-ahead.) I was positively glowing.

I was given a 10:00 PM curfew, so I had to make each minute matter. I'll never forget that night. As we got to his house, he held my hand and guided me to his basement bedroom. As we vibed out to Dave Matthews, he showed me his display of football trophies. He was peacocking for *me*, and it was utterly endearing.

We lay on his bed and started making out . . . and suddenly there *it* was. I'd never felt *it* before and tried to mask my uncertainty. If you don't know what an OTPHJ is, you should. (I'll give you a hint: Over the Pants Hand Job.) What was I supposed to do with *it*?

I reached down and fumbled around, thinking I was in the wrong place. Then I felt it . . . I think. So, I started petting it, the way one would pet a dog. I did this for what seemed like an eternity, until he lifted my hand away to offer some guidance . . . and *next thing you know it was skin on skin.* Finally!

I touched his penis! Now I could start planning our wedding!

Our destination wedding would be our high school colors, black and white—tuxedo colors! I was head over heels and we were 100 percent getting married. I knew we were young, but we would make it work.

The next day at school I told everyone about our

PLEASE JOIN US IN CELEBRATING

Kristen Doute

&

Her Cousin's Best Friend's Sister's Neighbor

ARE GETTING MARRIED!

deep love and that I now had a boyfriend. He, on the other hand, would only stop long enough to high-five me in the hallway between classes.

When we did finally have a moment alone together out by the bleachers after school, he told me to stop talking about what happened. He wanted us to be a secret. Something only we shared, just between us. At first, I was confused. Was he embarrassed of me? Did he have other secret girl rendezvous? I couldn't let him see how much this bothered me. I did what any mature high school girl would do. I flipped him two birds and I made sure to tell the rest of the school everything.

I didn't have time to waste on him. I didn't need or want to date a guy who didn't want to show me off. I knew I deserved a real relationship, out in public, in all its glory.

My First

WHEN A MAN DRIVES you crazy, sometimes you have to chase him.

The year was 1998. I was a sophomore. He was a senior. And it was time—time to lose my virginity. Here's how I did it.

PRO-TIP 1: *Choose Your Prey Wisely*

He was a hockey player. The quiet, mysterious type. He was just *different,* and he went to the other high school in our district, which made him even cooler. A novelty. He wasn't just one of the tired, same-old boys I'd grown up with, the ones I'd known since elementary school.

He had so much going for him, as far as I was concerned: he was two years older, he had this adorable dumb

21

haircut, and—most important—he had access to his parents' station wagon, which made everyone I knew *very* jealous.

I knew he was the one.

PRO-TIP 2: *Be Around Him . . . a Lot*

It's called the Propinquity Effect. Psychology 101. People are more likely to form relationships with someone they encounter often. The more frequently you see somebody, the more likely you are to forge a friendship with them—or start a romance.

But how to be around him when we went to different schools? Well, it turned out a girl could be the boys' hockey team manager. The only qualifications you really needed were: 1. being available, and 2. knowing how to count. I made myself extremely available and made sure I knew how to count points, goals, and assists.

Luckily for me we had one unified team for both district high schools, so there was only one team in the city. I couldn't skate, but I bought hockey skates anyway. I had a jersey made with his number on it, and took a leave of absence from my cheerleading squad.

I was all in.

We practiced four days a week, with games every Wednesday. *Nearness*, and lots of it. I had a whole season to work my wiles. On the way to Game 1, I got to sit next to him on the bus. After Game 2, we played pinball together at Hungry Howie's. By Game 7, I was taking mall trips with his sister. Halfway into the season? I was sharing mozzarella sticks with his parents, comparing our weekend plans.

PRO-TIP 3: *Don't Be Deterred by the Friend Zone*

Don't take "You're, like, my best friend" for an answer. Don't let him make you "like one of the guys." You can always turn that around. I did.

By the end of the season, we were thick as thieves. I invited him to our "Sponge" dance, our school's equivalent to a Sadie Hawkins dance. Girls were responsible for paying for the dance tickets, the corsages, everything; the guys "sponged" off the girls, hence the name. He accepted, but made sure to tell me we were just going as friends, of course. I knew I could change his mind.

I made my sister buy us a case of beer. I worked tirelessly on my dance moves. I bought the sickest dress from Jacobson's. Honestly, I think the case of beer alone would have done it. (I was a sophomore! That was impressive!)

I picked him up in our rented limo, and we chugged Natty Lights and drove around town—thirty minutes, just us, with no real direction. When we finally got to the dance, buzzed and excited, I felt the moment. I made my move. Lo and behold, my kiss was reciprocated. *Boom.* Did I have a boyfriend now?

PRO-TIP 4: *Create a Shared Near-Death Experience*

It's the all-time classic way to bond you and your man together. Just watch *The Bachelor* and *The Bachelorette*: Who do they always end up with? Whoever they take bungee jumping.

When the hockey team won the big game, high on victory, we all snuck out and went sledding. It was dark and scary, and we only had a flashlight and a two-person toboggan. He was the big spoon. First the kiss at the dance—incredible—and now I was wedged between his legs!

As we teetered on the top of the tallest hill, I could feel his heart pounding. He wanted to impress me. He wouldn't show fear, even though his palms were definitely sweating under those gloves that held me so tightly. He whispered, "You ready?"

I was.

We raced down the hill into the night, two people as one. We conquered our fears together, and I knew we would remember it for the rest of our lives.

PRO-TIP 5: *Always Be the Last to Leave*

We were in the basement, at his house, for the end-of-the-season party. His best friend said good-bye and left the two of us alone together. *Finally.*

The silence in the room was deafening. The clock ticked loudly on the wall.

10:01.

It was now or never.

There was no foreplay—we got right down to it. I was having sex for the first time. I felt myself drift to planning our wedding; I saw us in our little suburban bungalow, me in my business woman's outfit and him in his hockey jersey. He'd be a coach by then, or a pro—I was cool with either, really. It would be perfect. This was my husband-to-be.

I could see it all coming to fruition, and suddenly I felt the tears coming. *Fuck.*

I struggled to hold them back, to stay in the mood, but one tear slipped from my eye. I watched it as if it were moving in slow motion, falling from my gaze directly into his. Was this what it meant to share euphoria, together?

Why did I cry? I'm not sure. Was I happy because I was so excited? Was I sad because he wasn't my husband *yet*? Was I just crying because the floor was cold? The immensity of the situation hit me all at once, a subconscious flood of emotion.

I was so focused on plotting and planning that I didn't realize how my first time would feel. It was a tsunami. It *is* a big deal, and you don't understand how you'll feel until you're in the middle of it.

The salty tear hitting his eye startled him, and he pushed me to the side to seek refuge in his grandmother's knitted blanket. I glanced back at the clock.

10:02.

A magical minute.

PRO-TIP 6: *Memorialize It*

When summer came, he packed up for college. He was leaving town—leaving me. To honor our love, I made him a scrapbook filled with poems, song lyrics, and memories of our time together.

I will remember you, it said. *Will you remember me?*

I do, and he does. But it's just a memory. When he left, I was crushed, but I got over it.

Ladies, I promise you: we will *always* get over it.

He was never my boyfriend. We never had sex again. But he'll always be my first.

Something Intimate

HISTORICALLY, I HAVE A TYPE, and it's "dim-witted model boy." They've always ended up in my orbit. This particular one came disguised as a tire-changing manly man driving a yellow Mustang convertible. He was so striking that I overlooked his tongue ring, Hawaiian shirt, and lack of biceps.

Let me paint the picture for you: I was leaning dejectedly against my friend's broken-down Ford Taurus in a sundress that was probably too short for me to wear to school that day. We had just picked up her boyfriend from the rival high school, and all of the rich kids from his school kept whizzing by our defective vehicle, screaming expletives out their windows as they headed to Cedar Point, which is where we were *supposed* to be going.

My friend's boyfriend called his older brother to come and save the day. I couldn't be bothered. He wasn't arriving fast enough. I was uber annoyed and furious at this flat tire that was ruining my long-awaited half-day. Suddenly, like a hymn from heaven above, I heard DMX bumping and I jumped to attention. What was this vision, skidding around the corner in a hot rod? It was my chariot. My chariot drowning in Ruff Ryder rap. I was already drooling, and I began handing him his tools as he fixed the tire.

He was a senior and nineteen years old instead of eighteen . . . what did *that* mean? Well, it meant he'd probably failed a grade, but hell, he could get tattoos and piercings and he could drink legally across the border in Canada. I didn't know anyone else that could do that. Forget Cedar Point—my roller coaster for the next four months had arrived.

From that day forward, every waking moment, we were together. And by together, I mean we were having sex.

"Mom, we're going to a movie, be back soon." *Read:* We're having sex on the side of a dirt road.

"Mom, we're off to get some ice cream!" *Read:* We're having sex in the parking lot of a strip mall.

"Mom, we're going to Ram's Horn for French fries and ranch dressing!" *Read:* We're going to Ram's Horn for French fries and ranch dressing. That shit was good, and we needed sustenance for all the sexin' we were doing.

He was only the second guy I'd had sex with; he was the first person I'd slept with more than once. He was my actual boyfriend. This was adulting! For the first time in my life I knew that this relationship wasn't bullshit—this was real love. We were going to be together forever . . . until out of nowhere, this polarized-Oakley-wearing asshat tells me he's going to the University of Miami in the fall. *He* was accepted to a four-year college?

It turned out he wasn't a grade failer; he was a late grade *starter.* Apparently, some rich kids start school a year late to give them a leg up in getting into a better college. If I had done that, maybe I would've gotten into Harvard instead of working at SUR for seven years. We'll never know. I feel much smarter this year than I did last year, so the concept totally makes sense.

To be honest, the idea of having a college boyfriend was pretty exciting. I couldn't wait to rock his collegiate colors. I couldn't wait to go visit him and go to all the college parties, and I couldn't wait to apply to Miami too.

The day he left was the saddest day of my life up to that point. At that age, having what I thought was an adult relationship, doing adult things, with adult feelings, I didn't think I could ever live without him. My knowledge of his existence made it impossible. We promised to call each other every night. We promised to write letters every week. We promised nothing would change. Then, of course, everything changed.

Thanksgiving rolled around and he strolled back into town wearing a crisp white polo shirt and khaki pants, driving around in a burgundy SAAB with his new "Elle from *Legally Blonde* look alike" girlfriend. *As if!* I couldn't understand how he moved on so quickly. While he was going to sorority formals with Elle, I was going with groups of girlfriends to homecoming, pinning a picture of him to my strapless dress to make sure everyone knew I was off-limits.

What about our memories? We made *love.* We cuddled and talked for hours about life, our dreams, our future. There was no way I could wrap my head around the fact that he was sharing what *we* had shared together with someone else.

I never, in a million years, thought it would end. Ever—especially this way. What I thought we shared was unabashed affection with no fear whatsoever. I thought we shared mutual vulnerability. But he pulled a disappearing act. He didn't even have the courage to break up with me or to have a conversation about it. I was never given even a moment of opportunity to express how I felt, have those feelings acknowledged, or convey what I was going through. He only thought about himself. From then on, moving forward, the fear of losing anyone the way I lost him would keep me from that pure intimacy I'd been striving for.

The Thespian

'TWAS THE SEASON OF love. My dad was on to his second life with his soon-to-be new wife. Wedding bells were ring- ing. With the nuptials two months away, I was fantasizing about who would be standing next to me in my periwinkle-blue junior bridesmaid's dress.

There was this guy in high school that was in love with me. He was a *Thespian*. If you've never had a Thespian in love with you, you should know that it is very intense. I mentioned *once* that I liked the movie *Ace Ventura*. From that point on he ended every conversation with "All righty then." He made a lot of grandiose overtures to show me how much he adored me. He was, if nothing else, engaged. I figured, why not? I guess I'll give this theater kid a whirl. None of my other prospects seemed promising.

After agreeing to a Halloween couple's costume, finding poems in my locker, and listening to him serenade me with "This I Promise You" by *NSYNC, I had actually almost reached my limit. But then I went to see him in the school's rendition of *Grease*. He played Danny Zuko. And he was *divine*. That's when the flip happened. Now, I was enamored with *him*. It took one performance of "Greased Lightning" and I turned into Sandra Dee, batting my eyes. I didn't even like him five minutes ago and now he was *my man*.

One month, thirteen days, and seven minutes later, as I was getting my updo perfected for my dad's wedding, all I could think about was slow dancing with my Thespian at the reception. Was I going to get engaged tonight? We had a cool little tête-à-tête planned for after my walk down the aisle. I'd turn at the bottom of the altar, kick ball change into a side step as Lonestar's "Amazed" echoed through the church.

As I turned to seek out my Thespian (meant to be in the second row behind my grandparents), I found his seat mysteriously empty. Empty . . . bare . . . uninhabited . . . No. One. There. He ditched out! That twenty-minute Catholic service seemed to last as long as Moses wandering through the deserts after the Ten Plagues.

There was a smidgen of downtime between the photos and the reception during the adult cocktail hour, and I was going to go get him. I would *not* be stood up!

There was a limo. Granted, it was my dad's rented limo for the "just married, driving away as we all throw rice" finale, but it was the only mode of transportation available to me, so I took it. I hijacked the limo and demanded that the driver take me to confront my Thespian. It sounds crazy, because it is.

I had *just* allowed him to love me. He *loved me*—why would he not show up?

He answered the door in his smoking jacket and dress socks; he'd probably been lounging around watching John Waters's *Cry Baby* during my panic attack. My Thespian said he "got grounded" and couldn't come. OK. I hiked up my dress, pushed open the front door, and stormed in demanding to speak to his mother. I *knew* he was lying.

His mom came to the door, and I could tell right away that she was in on getting him out of it. To this day I refuse to believe he was ever grounded. (She would never do that to me, right? Ugh, but she *would* lie for him.) It was the first time I wore mascara; it ran down my cheeks.

Fuck the season of love.

Cheater

MY SENIOR YEAR WAS idyllic. A magical time. Everything was perfect. *He* was the star quarterback and *I* was a cheerleader. *Pleasantville* had nothing on the perfection that was my life.

He was gorgeous, with a perfect jawline and the biceps of a Greek god. He wasn't the brightest crayon in the box, sure, but my God was he adorable—a ditz, but in the cutest way. He was always happy, always smiling, and we always had fun together. We were two peas in a pod, with chemistry like I'd never felt before.

Bonus: he had three sisters, so he knew how to treat a lady (or, in this case, me); he was such a gentleman! On *our* dates, chivalry was not dead. He opened the door, he held my hand, and he *never* let me walk on the curb side of the street. We would go to Wendy's for Frosties and fries (he always saved the last fry for me) and then have date night at the cinema. Our kids were going to be tall, athletic, and gorgeous. I swooned over my own daydreams of marrying my high school sweetheart. We were going to be a success story.

Then one night my friend threw a house party while her parents were out of town. Like any good senior in high school at that time, I got completely hammered on Zima. I don't recommend a six-pack of malt liquor to *anyone*, much less a seventeen-year-old weighing in at 110 pounds. I got so sick I called it an early night and went home.

After five minutes of lying in bed, I got my bearings and my sixth sense kicked in. I remembered that I had left my quarterback and our friends with this girl who was *totally* obsessed with him. Back then we didn't have cell phones, so I couldn't blow him up with texts all night—I had to stalk him in person. The adrenaline rush made me feel like Superwoman. I washed my face, laced up my sneakers, and walked seventeen blocks back to the party—past three stop lights, a 7-Eleven, and a party store.

When I entered the living room, panic set in. *Where was he?* I immediately cross-examined the partygoers, inquiring where the hell he was. I knew my suspicions had been validated when they all had completely different, simultaneous answers: "He's in the bathroom!" "He went home!" "He ran to the store!" All in unison.

Something was up.

WHERE WAS HE?

WHERE WAS *SHE*?

I darted up to the second story, fought his best friend to the top of the stairs, and flipped on the light switch. There they were. Butt naked. In bed. Missionary position. I had caught him in bed with another girl. I ran hysterically down the stairs, locked myself in the bathroom, and began sobbing uncontrollably.

As I waited for him to kick down the door and drop to his knees to beg for forgiveness, filled with regret, acknowledging his terrible offense, the minutes ticked by. Eventually I got up from my fetal position and turned to look at myself in the bathroom mirror.

Have you ever looked at yourself in the mirror while ugly crying? It's embarrassing. It's like your reflection is mocking you. Try it sometime—it will make you stop crying instantly.

Why was *I* going full waterworks while he was upstairs still fucking another girl? And why was this apology taking twenty minutes? Why was *I* the one that had run out of that bedroom? *Oh, hell no.* I was going back to confront him! And as fate would have it, just as I finally exited the bathroom they were scurrying down the stairs.

I followed after him and he started acting as if he were some UFC referee, blocking me from getting to her. *Her?* I didn't care about *her. He* was the problem—he was *my* boyfriend.

In the heat of the moment, he called me a bitch—and so, in the heat of the moment, my fist connected with his nose.

It was a quick jab from the elbow, like in that *Donkey*

Kong video game. I don't know what came over me. I had never hit *anyone* in my life, and now there was blood all over my shirt. I was terrified.

We didn't talk all weekend. On Monday he came to school with two black eyes. We could have tried to stay together, but it would never be the same. It was impossible to continue dating when my new nickname around school was "Tyson." His parents wanted to press charges. The appeal of a forbidden love could only last so long.

Before this incident, the concept of cheating—like *that*—had never even occurred to me. Why would someone cheat? Why wouldn't they just break it off? Wouldn't I know that something was wrong with our relationship before catching him in the act with someone else?

I had to reevaluate, regroup, and rebound. How could I be so naive? *I could never let this happen again.*

Crazy Kristen had awakened.

PART TWO

Kissing Every Frog

Detective Doute

IN 2003, AS I WAS TURNING twenty years old, I was in my longest relationship to date. My boyfriend and I had been together for two years, and on a scale from one to peak Crazy Kristen, I was still a somewhat trusting, normal human being.

So it starts off like this: he was going on a family cruise. *Extended* family, so we're talking siblings, stepsiblings, parents, grandparents, uncles, aunts, the whole shebang. Cool, whatever; I had no worries. I had zero reason in the world to think he would be shady, to think he would cheat, to think he would even *talk* to another girl. We were in *love*. It had been two years and everything was *perfect*. Famous last words.

On night three of the cruise, I got this really strange call on my mom's landline. (A call on a landline, obviously, is monumental and memorable.) On the other end of the line is a friend of mine, and she tells me her boyfriend's cousin is on the same cruise.

What are the odds? They're in Mexico, and we live in Michigan, but this guy happens to be on the ship and he says he saw my boyfriend "canoodling" with a younger girl.

OK, Kristen, calm down. His stepsister is in high school. Maybe he was hugging her, or taking a photo with her. Who knows!

My gut told me it wasn't true and I had nothing to worry about . . . so I blew it off. (So much for women's intuition!) Still, I kept the information stored away in my back pocket. That's sort of my MO—I keep things close and lie in wait.

When he got back from the cruise, he suddenly had to go on a business trip to Atlanta with his father and his uncle. My reaction: "Really, bro?" It didn't sit right with me; he had *just* come back, and I wanted to spend time with him. But for some reason, at this early stage, my brain didn't immediately go to his alleged *cruise canoodle.*

The next morning, he was supposedly gone to Atlanta. But the moment I woke up I felt it. My women's intuition coming through, at last.

Something is wrong. SOMETHING is fucked up.

Let's fucking go.

It was time to get to the bottom of this, and Detective Doute was on the case.

For better or worse, here's how I cracked it:

STEP 1: *Confirm the Lie*

The first thing to do is make sure your man is actually lying. Luckily, in this instance, I happened to be working for his family's carpet cleaning business. I was the receptionist, so I knew that if I called the office line during this business trip—a "carpet cleaning convention," allegedly—there'd be no one there to answer the call. Apart from me, the only people who worked there were my boyfriend, his father, and his uncle. All were in Atlanta, or so I'd been told.

So I called. Once I hit four rings I felt terrible, immediately regretting not trusting him. In my mind's eye I was on my knees, baking him "please forgive me" cookies . . . and then his uncle answered the phone. "Hello?"

What. The. *Fuck*.

"Hi, um, this is Kristen! I thought you guys were in Atlanta for the carpet cleaning convention?"

He stumbled over his words, knowing he'd been caught, knowing he'd exposed his nephew in a lie. *MEN*. "Uh, er, oh. Well . . ."

I couldn't even hear what he was mumbling. I was seeing red.

My boyfriend had *lied* to me. It was now 100 percent on.

STEP 2: *Catch Him in the Act*

Time to call your best friend. You'll need someone to drive you, because you will be too busy ranting about what you're going to do to your boyfriend when you see him.

I called one of my girlfriends, sobbing and spewing venom, and she said, "Hold up. We don't cry, we get even. Let's just go to his house and see. It's only like thirty minutes from here."

So, we did. Right when we pulled up I saw his car, a stupid red Pontiac Sunfire with a giant Cobra Starship bumper sticker. Behind it sat another car, with a Pennsylvania license plate. I definitely did not know that car. I definitely did not know anyone from Pennsylvania. All I knew in that moment was that when I walked in I'd better find his random cousin in from out of town, some long-lost relative visiting from Pittsburgh.

I casually stomped up the driveway to the side door. It was locked. As I peered into the window I saw him on the couch in the living room, lying there with *a girl*. I started banging on the door like a full-on bunny boiler.

He ran out, slammed the door behind him, and started yelling at *me*! The audacity. Through my rage blackout I vividly remember him whining, "What the hell are you doing here?" Men *often* behave like this to deflect when caught.

Ugh, typical.

I remember him throwing a trash can and throwing a tantrum, as though *I* were the one who'd done something wrong here. So I just left.

How was your *carpet cleaning convention*, bro? And who is that little skank on the couch?

STEP 3: *Get Wasted. Vow to Never Speak to Him Again*

Young Kristen was so naive. But I had a bottle of Mohawk Vodka, a Slurpee, and my friends, so I knew I was going to be fine. I got wasted with my Girl Squad at home and we blathered on about all his shortcomings: *Screw* his soccer player calves! *Screw* his upper lip freckle! I didn't even *really* like him in the first place!

He was blowing up my phone all night, calling every three seconds. His voicemails were pathetic and repetitive. "I love you," he said. "I'm so sorry," he said.

Blah, blah, blah! Give me a break. I'm not *that* stupid. Who do you think you are?

STEP 4: *Remember the Good Times. Doubt Your Own Eyes*

The next morning, with the Girl Squad gone and the spiked Slurpee haze wearing off, I listened to his messages again. With fresh ears, the voicemails weren't at all pathetic—they were *ah-mazing*. He was owning up to it! He explained that she seduced him. He repeatedly told her he had a girlfriend but she wouldn't take no for an answer. Maybe it wasn't his fault.

It made me think of all the reasons we were together in the first place. How I'd been so lucky to find this wonderful man right after graduating from high school. How he'd taught me to play guitar. How just recently we'd discussed moving in together. How I was *killing it* at my job as a receptionist at a carpet cleaning company, his *family's* carpet cleaning company, the carpet cleaning company we were going to own together one day. It would be perfect. This was my husband-to-be. All of my friends had gone off to college and were working toward degrees. I didn't know which direction I wanted my life to go. At the time I thought marrying *him* and having a stable job that was parallel to *his* career equaled success and happiness.

Maybe I'd overreacted. Did I *really* see what I thought I saw, there on that couch? Did my eyes deceive me?

STEP 5: *Blame Her. Forgive Him*

You know how girls are! SHE seduced him. SHE drove twelve hours to visit a complete stranger she kissed once on some stupid cruise. SHE was the problem. She had *pressured* him until he cracked. She *knew* he had a serious girlfriend and pursued him anyway. She was a *devil woman* and obviously not a girl's girl.

She had trapped my man and single-handedly tried to ruin my life. But she had failed! We were solid again, he and I. We had a long heart-to-heart over the phone, and he promised me he'd kicked her out of his house and she was gone forever.

STEP 6: *Catch Him, Again*

Two hours later.

In my fantasy he was driving over immediately to check on me, with a bouquet of roses so extravagant it was disgusting.

Every minute that passed without him turning up felt like an eternity—an eternity of being stabbed in the heart with fiery swords. Where *was* he?

I called that same girlfriend to come over to console me again, as she only lived like two blocks away. Suddenly I could feel it in my bones. Adrenaline flooding my body, I started ranting to her. "I don't know why, but he said that she left, and I think that he's lying!"

She grabbed her keys and my coat and said the magic words: "Do we wanna go back over there?"

I sure as hell did.

Round two, another thirty-minute drive. Off we went. This wasn't over.

I didn't call ahead, we just drove. I *had* to know. Lo and behold the Pennsylvania license plate car was still in the driveway. They had been cooped up snuggling all weekend long! *Precious.* I went to the side door again, but this time they weren't in the living room.

He had left the door unlocked. *Idiot.*

Did I go in? Of course I went in.

I beelined straight to his bedroom, threw open the door, and found them lying in bed together, under the covers. *CANOODLING!* I ripped off the blankets, screaming, and thankfully they were wearing pajamas.

(I hadn't really thought that one through. What if they had been naked? I don't know what I would have done. I conceivably could have committed murder. My life would have gone in a very different direction, with a life sentence at the Women's Huron Valley Correctional Facility instead of a starring role on *Vanderpump Rules.* Same diff? Maybe.)

Anyway, he immediately jumped up and ran out of the room. *Coward.* He legit left me alone in the room with her! I was ready to punch a girl for the first time. In my head I was chanting *girl fight, girl fight* over and over, trying to amp myself up until I had the courage to take a swing.

I was about to do it when she gazed up at me. Full transparency . . . she just seemed kind of weird. This poor girl. I decided I wasn't going to get in a physical fight with somebody who just *stared* like that, who didn't seem like she would fight back. She just lay there, blinking at me way too slowly for comfort. So I left.

STEP 7: *Forget Everything. He's the One!*

A few days later, in a moment of weakness, I took him back. Like an idiot.

Sue me. I'm not perfect!

STEP 8: *Let Your Suspicions Grow*

After a mental week hiatus, I came back to work at his family's business again, but he and his father and his uncle were always out doing something—cleaning carpets, I guess!—and I was left sitting in front of a computer at reception all day long.

Listen, the future belongs to the curious.

Over time that nagging voice in the back of my head told me something just wasn't right. I felt this crazy urge to hack into his email. So . . . I did.

STEP 9: *Discover His Secrets*

The thing about emails is that there are a *lot* of folders to sift through.

First I went through his inbox, and when I didn't find anything there I went to his sent emails . . . then his *deleted* sent emails, in the trash. Her name started flashing on the screen before my eyes. *Son of a bitch*, they were still in touch. *Still!*

I didn't say anything to him. I just went right to work.

STEP 10: *Destroy Him. And Her*

Remember, babes, this was back in the early aughts, when we didn't have the same technology we have now. We didn't have Instagrams to stalk, or smartphones to pore over, so I had to do some real digging.

LiveJournal was big back then—if you're too young to remember, it was like a live diary, almost like Tumblr or Twitter, and your friends could comment on your journal entries. I started Googling this girl based on the Hotmail address I'd found in his deleted emails. Soon enough her LiveJournal popped up, where she boringly talked about her two cats that she loved so much.

I knew this would be the easiest email hack ever. Her first security question: "What is your pet's name?" Two guesses and I was in.

After this momentous CIA-level achievement, with access to her account the first thing I had to do was change all of her security questions. I couldn't risk her logging in during my victory lap! I changed her birthday and all of her personal information, making sure she could not possibly get back into her email.

As the final nail in her coffin I did what any respectable boss bitch would do: I broke up with him, as her, via her email address. And I told him he should probably go to the clinic and get checked out. I blocked him, deleted her LiveJournal, and signed her up for a million spam sites. I left a note on the hood of his stupid Sunfire, telling him he and I were over for good.

It's important to be thorough.

Password Questionnaire

When you're dating someone, you want to ask a lot of "natural" questions that don't seem too invasive. Ice-breakers! The key, though, is to make sure you choose your questions wisely—because you are actually gathering important information.

The conversation should go something like this:

You: What kind of music do you listen to?

Him: Blah, blah, blah. (*You don't actually care*)

You: What was your first concert? Do you even remember?

Him: Red Hot Chili Peppers. (*File this away*)

You: Mine was New Kids on the Block! But that's really funny, actually, because my sixth-grade teacher's nickname was Flea. Like, how random is that? (*this is not even true*)

Him: So random!

You: I even remember my first-grade teacher's name: Ms. Leslie. There's no way *you* remember your first-grade teacher's name.

Him: I do! It was Ms. Jackie. (*Bingo.*)

You: Shut up! You have, like, the *best* memory.
Did you play sports in high school? I was a
cheerleader. (*This one is true*) We were the
Thunderbirds.

Him: We were the Bobcats! I played basketball.

Keep this up until you also have the following
potential security questions answered:

- First Pet / Current Pet
- First Girlfriend's Name
- First Car
- City Where He Was Born
- Middle Name
- Father's Middle Name
- Mother's Maiden Name

These are rapid-fire, simple fifteen to twenty
questions that you just spit out when you're getting
to know your new guy. There doesn't have to be a
rhyme or reason as to why you're asking. You are on
a fact-finding mission, and he'll ask you what your
answers are, too. The difference? He just wants to
actually get to know you.

File these away for a rainy day.

You're welcome.

Three's a Crowd

IT WAS ABOUT THREE months after I'd left the cheating heir to the carpet cleaning business, and sure, maybe I wasn't ready to jump into another long-term relationship. And, yeah, all right, *maybe* I was still dealing with some PTSD from the whole thing, from Pennsylvania Girl's weird fish-eyed stare and stupid Lip Freckle Dude's stupid lip freckle.

But suddenly, here he was: my new knight in shining armor. You can't choose when you meet the one!

He walked into the bar with a sleeve tattoo, a newsboy cap, and a smile to die for. He was a full-on Burner and he loved EDM. (I didn't know what EDM was, but I now loved EDM as well.) He was a DJ, and by DJ I mean he made mash-ups. He liked to paint. No real job, no real direction—a free spirit. An *artist*. How could this go wrong?

Ten days after we met, he told me he was moving to Ocean City, Maryland, to DJ at some beach bar. They were giving him a free condo, and he wanted me to come stay with him. I was twenty-two years old and I hadn't been anywhere. Like, I'd been to Disney World, but that was about it. Ten days into our relationship, we were already saying "I love you." I booked the next flight out to join him with the remainder of the carpet cleaning money I'd earned.

I thought we would be living the dream, but we were *so* broke. Like, a box of pancake mix had to last a week broke. Just to stay afloat, I started waiting tables at the same beach club where he was DJing. This bar, not known for being super classy, was—get this—*in* the ocean. Literally in the ocean. Like, big rafts and high-top tables—*in the ocean*—with seaweed, crabs, and jellyfish. As the new girl, I was given the deep end.

The red bikini and fanny pack they gave me as a uniform didn't exactly help me get over my extreme fear of the water, but I tried to see the bright side: at least I would be right next to him.

My second week in, my big toe got bit by a fucking crab.

I bolted out of that bay like an Olympic track star and *quit*. I would do anything for love, but I won't do crabs.

But he was so mature about the crab ordeal, so understanding! And there were plenty of other ways for us to make a living. We did what anyone else would do, obviously: we started a band. One dollar for a permit—just four quarters!—and we were the latest attraction on the boardwalk, living the dream. I played my six-string; he played harmonica and freestyled. He couldn't do either of those things very well, but at the time I thought that it was endearing.

I quickly learned, though, that dating a "rock star" came with downsides. The stereotype rang true: massive ego, deluded (he thought he could *rap*!), reckless, and he drank . . . *a lot*. Dirty Bananas for breakfast, Rum Runners for lunch; he never met a frozen concoction he didn't like.

Days turned into nights . . . nights when he was arrested by a horse cop while freestyling, nights when he was dragged in handcuffs down the boardwalk, and nights when he wouldn't even come home at all. To top it all off, he was still working at the beach bar after I quit, and a hot new waitress had turned up. They spent every night together, and I spent every night trying and failing to meet up with them. The most infuriating part? They had *inside jokes*.

They were clearly fucking, and I had a plan to prove it.

I decided we were going to have a threesome. I'd never had a threesome before, but I *knew* that it would give me the answers I needed. Watching them together, how they interacted sexually, I would be able to tell that they had hooked up before. This 100 percent made sense to me at the time—a foolproof scheme, a brilliant strategy.

His birthday was coming up, which was the perfect opportunity. (A bonus: I didn't have to buy him a gift! Two birds, one stone.) Five Long Island iced teas and six tequila shots into the birthday party, Hot Waitress was acting too nice, too interested, and too attentive . . . to *me*. Was she running a con on me? Pulling the old "act like you're my best friend while you're fucking my boyfriend behind my back" act?

I was wasted, finally hammered enough to muster up the courage and lead the threesome charge. We stumbled back to her place . . . and I didn't have to do a damn thing. *She* kissed *me*. *Only* me. I tried to turn our attention to the birthday boy, but she kept initiating only with me. It became crystal clear, all at once, that *I* was the object of her affection, not my boyfriend. They had never laid a finger on one another.

My radar had been completely off. I found out exactly what I needed to know. He was completely faithful to me. Time to abort mission!

I excused myself to the bathroom, grabbed my boyfriend's hand, and dragged him with me. He wanted to stay but I told him the drinks were *really* hitting me and I needed to go home immediately. We stumbled awkwardly back through her bedroom and out the front door, waving good-bye. I don't think she even noticed or cared that we were leaving.

Summer was winding down and the city was turning into a ghost town. Our friend group was dwindling, some going back home and some moving on to greener pastures. We had a huge going away party for everyone at our favorite bar, Peppers Tavern. My boyfriend and Hot Waitress left together early, tired. No big deal. I'd definitely established there was nothing between them. It was my last night too, and I wanted to party!

I stumbled home at 4:00 AM only to find an empty condo and a letter wedged in our screen door. He broke up with me in a fucking *note*.

The note said, and I quote: "I didn't realize how much [Hot Waitress] meant to me and how amazing our friendship was. It really was the basis for a fruitful relationship. Thanks for the great times. We had a good run."

Whatever, dude. If I'd gone for it, she would've left with *me*.

Nonconsensual

WE WERE ACQUAINTANCES. We partied together.

When I sat down to map out my book, at first I didn't want to write about this. Overall this book is supposed to be fun and tongue-in-cheek, with humorous dating stories that poke a little fun at myself and also call out the men who've done me wrong.

I have never discussed this publicly before.

But I wouldn't be speaking my whole truth if I didn't include it in here somehow. I feel the need to address it. I wouldn't be being completely vulnerable and honest with you if I chose not to include it. I don't know if it's something that has scarred me for life, or something I'll eventually move beyond for good. In the past I've always tried to justify what happened to me by telling myself that it wasn't *that* bad.

It's sad how I tried to justify it to myself after I had been violated. Just because it wasn't "violent" and no weapon was used, or anything like that, I told myself that it didn't rise to the level where it should be considered rape. But it *was* rape.

I tried to let it go.

But the more we allow this kind of behavior to be swept under the rug, the more we allow ourselves not to talk about it, the more this will keep happening to other women.

It has to stop.

Date rape is rape. It's time we take out the word "date"; that's just there to minimize it. I don't think about what happened to me often, but when I do, I cry. I know that means it did have an effect on me, and that it does still affect who I am today.

This is something that I have to live with forever. I'm sure he doesn't even remember the incident at all.

I know too many girls that this has happened to. I'm sure you do, too. I'm not going to go into intricate details of my story, but I do want to talk about my experience. This topic can be so taboo, and I think it's crucial not to skate by it.

After this happened to me, I felt immense shame. I was so angry, I wanted to kill this person. But I didn't want to tell anyone, because I was worried that no one would believe me. I was afraid that people would say I put myself in that situation, rather than blaming him for knowing I was too impaired at the time to make a conscious choice.

Once things started to really sink in, I began to feel guilty—about the possibility of ruining *his* life. About ruining friendships we shared. I felt like I'd be causing trouble. It's sad, but this is the reality of what a lot of women feel when this happens to us.

This created a lot of long-standing trust issues for me. I tried to convince myself that if I hadn't been *irresponsible*, if I hadn't drunk so much, it wouldn't have happened to me. I hoped I could will these feelings away, the feelings of knowing that I said NO but had somehow "allowed" it to happen anyway.

But what if this man did this to other girls?

Just because I didn't have to physically fight him off doesn't mean what happened is OK. This man, single-handedly, made me feel disgusting in my own skin.

If a girl's too drunk, leave her alone. If she is unable to consent, leave her alone. When she says no, leave her alone.

It takes an insane amount of courage to speak out and report it. There are lots of reasons why people are afraid to report. At the time, I wasn't brave enough, but I beg you to be brave. It's not your fault, no matter what.

That kind of predatory behavior from men needs to stop. Now.

Only Skin Deep

I HAD ONLY LIVED in L.A. for a couple months when I met a new guy. A few of my girlfriends and I were at a dive bar when this hot tattooed chick approached me at the bar and asked if I was single. Was she hitting on me? She was stunning, and I wasn't totally against it, but I was still a little scarred from that humiliating threesome fail with Hot Waitress from the beach bar.

She wasn't asking for herself, though, it turned out. A male friend of hers thought I was hot, but he was too shy to approach me. She introduced us and it was lust at first sight. I was crushing *hard*. He was tan with light eyes and covered in tattoos. It was a hipster bar but he was too *cool* to be just a hipster—*he* was a touring drum tech for a big rock band. Oh, *My So-Called Life*. I was dying to be in the music industry and he was exactly the type of guy I was hoping to meet in Los Angeles.

63

Two weeks after we met, he had to leave for tour. I drove him to LAX, parked my car in the lot across the street, and escorted him to the Tom Bradley International Terminal to say our good-byes. I knew we would reconnect in four weeks but I still couldn't hide my tears. He kissed my forehead, said, "I'll see ya soon," and jetted off.

We dated for a couple of months, and though he was mostly in Japan and Australia we texted almost every day. He would send me selfies from Sydney and Skype me from Tokyo. My long-distance boyfriend was extremely attentive.

He finally came back from tour just before the holidays, but I was heading back to Michigan for Christmas! Ugh, timing. I missed him so much.

Then he invited me to spend New Year's Eve at his sister's house with his parents, nieces, and nephews. We had a Disney-themed party for the kids, and I was more than happy to be hanging with my hot boyfriend rather than out raging with my friends.

Kid parties end early, thank God, and we made it back to my apartment just before the ball dropped. We needed to start off the new year with a bang, and as the clock struck 12:00 we clinked our Corona Lights, he kissed me, and I tossed a handful of confetti.

One minute later, at exactly 12:01, he paused, looked me in the eye, and said, "I can't do this anymore."

I reached for his beer and told him I got it, because I didn't really want to drink anymore either!

"No," he said. "I don't want to date you."

I was stunned. "You're breaking up with me?" He was breaking up with me in the first minute of January? What kind of monster *does* that?

Then, the real kicker: he said he couldn't be breaking up with me if he was never officially my boyfriend.

WHAT?

This had to be about *the tattoo*.

Let me tell you about this tattoo: it was a series of four tiny stars wreathed in ivy that he drew himself, inked on his beautiful forearm. It was a lovely sight that I woke up to whenever we woke up together (a grand total of two times). I just knew he always wanted me to get a matching one. This *had* to be why he broke up with me.

I texted my tattoo artist friend in Hollywood begging her to ink me in the morning. I didn't have a photo of the tattoo on my phone, but I didn't need one—I could draw it for her by memory. That was etched in my brain. *I'll show him the tattoo, he'll take me back, take me on tour with him—first stop: Toronto!* I was great at taking direction and could totally be his roadie. I just needed to get a passport.

I hatched a scheme to *randomly* run into him at the Burgundy Room on the Wednesday night I knew his friend was bartending.

Listen, you can't scheme all by yourself. If you're not already out, you at least need to act like you have been—dressed to the nines, *some* makeup, and your girl posse ready to party. So I made sure I looked great and made sure I had backup.

When we walked in, I saw him at the end of the bar and beelined straight for him. I ordered my drink, extending my left arm to make sure my freshly tattooed wrist was in his eye line.

It wasn't quite the reaction I expected. He was nice . . . but said, "Why would you do that?"

He definitely never explicitly asked or told me to get this tattoo. He *maybe* said something like "this would look cute on you" after I said I liked it. I had 100 percent extrapolated the rest.

And now I had engraved my most fleeting non-relationship relationship as a permanent fixture on my wrist. The irony was not lost on me. Unfortunately for me, I had to carry this embarrassing mistake around on my forearm for a whole month before I could get another tattoo to cover it.

I chose the symbol for Aquarius, my sun sign, as it represents the water from the vessel washing away the past and leaving room for a fresh new start.

The Five Kinds of Crazy

🦋 UNDERCOVER CRAZY

≥ What HE Thinks

1. This girl's chill.
2. My friends think she's chill.
3. We just have sex casually every once in a while, but she's definitely cool with it.

≥ Her Crazy TRUTH

1. This girl's crazy.
2. Your friends clocked her as crazy the first time they met her.
3. She's soooo not cool with it.

≥ Red Flag

She rarely wears underwear, but *does* wear her half of a matching friendship bracelet set she bought the both of you for your birthday.

🦋 TORCH-CARRYING CRAZY

≥ What HE Thinks

1. She's one of my oldest, bestest girlfriends from back home.
2. "I think we may have hooked up once in high school, maybe. . . ?"
3. My mom really likes her.

⋟ Her Crazy TRUTH

1. She has a cabinet full of notebooks with "Mrs. [His Last Name]" written over and over again.
2. She thinks you were her high school boyfriend.
3. She and your mom talk every day, on the phone, about you.

⋟ Red Flag

She wears your football jersey to bed, every night. She's never washed it. Ever.

🦋 FRIEND GROUP CRAZY

⋟ What HE Thinks

1. We have the same friends, and that's why she's always around.
2. She's actually into my best friend.
3. She gets free drinks for us at the bar . . . a lot.

⋟ Her Crazy TRUTH

1. She plans every group night out, and makes all your other friends ensure you turn up.
2. She doesn't even know your best friend.
3. She has a second job to pay for all the shots she buys for you.

⋟ Red Flag

She's always next to you in the group pictures and, although you didn't notice it before, she's never looking at the camera. Always at you.

❦ TRANSCENDENTAL CRAZY

⋛ What HE Thinks

1. I feel somehow drawn to her when she's around.
2. I sometimes dream about her.
3. When I pass a flower shop, my ring finger tingles.

⋛ The Crazy TRUTH

1. She put a spell on you, 1000%.

⋛ Red Flag

Seemingly insignificant items go missing from your house. You're missing a patch of hair.

❦ FULL-BLOWN CRAZY

⋛ What HE Thinks

1. She's good in the sack.
2. I can handle a little bit of crazy.

⋛ Her Crazy TRUTH

1. She's fantasized about leaving you tied up to her bed forever.
2. She fears no repercussions. One false move and you're her prisoner for life.

⋛ Red Flag

HER CRAZY EYES. Dead giveaway. You knew it! You knew it the first time you saw her but you played dumb! And you're still with her to this day, and we all know why. (SEE: "What HE Thinks," #1)

Double - Booked

BEFORE THERE WAS Tinder, Bumble, Coffee Meets Bagel, Hinge, Happn, the League, or Raya . . . there was MySpace. It was *the* antiquated dating portal, if you're not familiar. If you're a bit younger you wouldn't believe the hours we spent on our wallpaper, curating the perfect song list, *ranking our top 8*; it was endless.

The "About Me" section was more crucial than your username. It was essentially your social résumé. It took me years to perfect mine, and I usually updated it on the reg. Luckily for you guys, I saved mine years ago. This was my final MySpace Manifesto:

TRÉS10
Wednesday, May 2, 200X 3:47 PM
Mood: Hopeful

ABOUT ME: MUSIC is my life. i am captured by quick wit and i love to laugh. i live in flip flops. i love to people watch, especially

71

when they don't know you're looking. i'm ridiculously indecisive. i have a serious fish phobia. i'm a future burner and stoked for BRC. i'm incredibly fortunate. "i've learned that even when i have pains, i don't have to be one." (M.A.) i don't always shut up but could sit and listen for hours. i LOVE football. i never litter. i am a terrible liar, but a good actress. i can't stand coffee. i'm a sponge - tell me something i don't know and teach me something worthwhile. i'm drawn toward cleverness and sarcasm (don't take life so damn seriously). i love fashion, style (particularly my own). i have the best friends in the world. i'm SUCH an aquarian. my guitar is my backbone . . . my way of venting on a bad day (or a really good one). ART! painting, picture taking, picture making . . . i create collages when i'm bored. i LOVE to travel - 2500 miles or roadtripping a few hours (and i have the best road trip partner ever). i dig good tunes on a long drive. go through life without regret - you live and you learn. i believe in karma (and sometimes it's a bitch). MAKE LOVE, NOT WAR. 4:20

TOP FRIEND:

Tom

I was single, living in Los Angeles, and I had a kick-ass MySpace persona. Why not search the site for guys in my new neighborhood? It was a treasure trove of single, hot men. That's how I met ValleyGuy.

My first date with ValleyGuy was at Runyon Canyon. Hiking seemed like a safe bet, so I met him there one afternoon. He was so attractive—like *man* attractive. I was used to dating *boys*. He would definitely age well. He was Russian and had grown up in the Valley. He was the type of guy who seemed like he would be in finance, and it turned out he was. He was completely different from anyone I had ever dated. He was a real adult, but somehow exactly my age.

Our dates were always daytime dates, because he worked from home. One might see this as a positive—*coffee* and not *cocktails*!—but I basically became his daytime booty call between meetings. He seemed to always be "busy" at night.

So who was his *nighttime* booty call? Did he have a girlfriend?

Around this time, I booked an acting job doing background work on the movie *He's Just Not That into You*, so I read the book it was based on. *Are you kidding me?* This was *exactly* what was happening to me.

Oh my God, ValleyGuy was Just Not That into Me.

So, while I was still semi-seeing ValleyGuy I started semi-seeing someone else—someone who seemed like a better prospect. I was not about to just wait around, hoping ValleyGuy would realize what a great catch I was. I mean, refer back to that MySpace *About Me*! I was clearly amazing.

This other guy, who I also met on MySpace, was the complete opposite of ValleyGuy. I can't remember his username, but we can just call him Zoolander.

Zoolander and I were nighttime partiers while ValleyGuy was my daytime lover. If I could've melded them into a two-headed boyfriend, they would have made the perfect partner. Sometimes, you just want to have it all. In this case, my attempt at playing the field fell short.

It's all about who's the distancer and who's the pursuer. Once I made myself less available, suddenly these commitmentphobes wanted a real relationship. ValleyGuy was eager for me to come to dinner with his clients, and Zoolander wanted to grab brunch during the day. I was playing hard to get mostly by accident, but my game was on point.

Around that time, I flew to Michigan for my cousin's wedding. I went solo. ValleyGuy found the wedding location and flew himself out there. He showed up to surprise me, and my entire family assumed he was my boyfriend, because only a boyfriend would make such a grand gesture. Where was *this* guy three months ago? I guess he really did love me now, but at this point I felt conflicted. I liked them both.

I should have told ValleyGuy right then that I was also seeing someone else. But . . . I didn't. When I was face to face with someone who had flown twenty-five hundred miles to proclaim his love in front of my family, I didn't want to hurt his feelings or his ego.

Back in L.A., things resumed as usual, but now there were feelings involved on all sides. I should have decided before shit hit the fan, but what was I supposed to do when I just *really liked* two different guys? I'd never been in this situation before.

Then . . . *shit hit the fan.*

Zoolander picked me up from work to confront me about my so-called player ways. Turns out he and ValleyGuy had been at the bar all night swapping war stories about me. Maybe I wasn't completely transparent with them, but I didn't lie to them either. And if neither of them wanted to be my exclusive boyfriend until *now* apparently, why did they care so much? *Great.* Now I was scared I was going to lose them both, but I wasn't prepared to have the conversation.

He dropped me off at home, and then they were both blowing up my cell phone at once, demanding that I make a choice. I didn't want to do that, so instead I did the obvious thing an irrational person would do: I poured myself a glass of vodka and took two Tylenol PMs.

Was I trying to get attention? Probably, subconsciously. But really, I was just trying to go to sleep and make it all go away for now.

I woke up to multiple firefighters lifting me out of bed and carrying me out of my apartment. *What the fuck was happening? Was the house on fire?* I remember demanding, in a panic, for them to let me go and tell me what was going on. As I was carried past my kicked-in front door and put on a stretcher into an ambulance, I saw ValleyGuy and Zoolander standing there together in front of my apartment building.

By the time I arrived at the hospital, I was fully sober. Evidently, I had passed out while I was on the phone with Zoolander, and one of them called 911.

I didn't mean to create this over-the-top incident, but as they both hovered over my hospital bed I couldn't help but hope maybe it would get me off the hook in terms of making the choice. It was wonderful to see how much they cared, but this wasn't exactly the way I wanted to find out they *were* both Actually That into Me. Or, at least, they had been.

This was my first and last attempt at dating two guys simultaneously without telling them. It turned out my MySpace manifesto was correct—karma is a bitch.

The Cult Classic

THE SEARCH FOR ENLIGHTENMENT takes center stage in your twenties, because *this cannot possibly be it*. I was broke, living in a tiny apartment, no real food, staying up all night and sleeping all day. I couldn't even afford a five-dollar footlong at Subway. I started questioning everything.

What's life all about? This question becomes the central topic of many late-night epiphany-induced conversations. Those nights I thought I had cracked the code, which became groggy mornings where I couldn't remember anything. *There* has *to be more, right?*

Luckily, in Los Angeles, it seemed like *everyone* was on a journey to find true enlightenment. Mostly we told ourselves that if we gave up just *one* three-day-weekend of wine and weed, we would be healed. Personally, I tried everything: self-help books, yoga, incense, crystals, incantations, *The Artist's Way*. I left no stone unturned (because that would have been bad feng shui). Even, as it turns out, a cult.

So basically, I started dating this guy. He was in a cult.

(It *is* Los Angeles, after all.)

It seemed pretty cult-y to me, anyway, but I didn't know for sure at the time. He was so very even-keeled, *loved* to communicate all of his feelings, and said things like "You don't make a decision, you make a choice." He advised me to "create my own possibility." We never fought—not because I didn't try, but because he refused to, even when I was hangry or PMSing. He always had this unwavering namaste attitude. Eventually I told him that his refusal to engage in arguments was making me feel insane. His solution? He enrolled me in the cult! An intensive weekend of self-discovery.

I should have told him to go straight to hell, but then he promised that after my graduation from the weekend course he'd take me on vacation with his family in Palm Springs. I had been dying to go to Palm Springs, *and* to meet his family.

The course was a three-day program in the middle of nowhere near LAX, with roughly 110 people in my class and two "leaders" who everyone said were the best coaches the program had to offer. I was going to be *transformed*. Allegedly.

THE CULTIFICATION OF KRISTEN: *Day 1*

6:00 AM. I was nervous. I wasn't sure what to expect but I was determined to start with an open mind. Mr. Namaste assured me that the twelve-hour days would be illuminating. *Twelve hours?* Pretty sure I was going to end up stabbing myself in the eye with a fork. Was I going to get a lunch break, or any break at all? Was starvation one of their tactics? I was about to find out . . .

He dropped me off on the curb at a nondescript office building, and I stood there feeling like that first day of kindergarten when you watch your parents drive off, afraid it's the last time you'll ever see them.

The room was cold. Only rows and rows and rows of chairs, fluorescent lights overhead, and water. That was it. I spotted an empty seat in the back row and sat down between two middle-aged men smack dab in the heart of their midlife crisis. One of the leaders immediately put me on blast for being late. I was *two minutes* late. He argued I was not "present." *Excuse me?* Calm down. I'm here. I'm literally present.

Was Palm Springs really worth this insanity? What had I gotten myself into?

We were given limited breaks, limited food, limited access to the real world. There were people there more than twice my age with a lifetime full of regrets they wanted absolved. I quickly knew I didn't belong there. During the first "group exercise" I beelined for the only other girl my age I could find, and *thank God* we immediately bonded. She was from Michigan, too. To this day, she's one of my besties.

I was happy that my new friend still had one foot firmly planted in reality with me, so that we could endure seventy-two hours of brainwashing together.

But I will admit, by the end of the day I had witnessed a few of the other students having real breakthroughs and wondered if some of these teachings could potentially benefit me.

THE CULTIFICATION OF KRISTEN: *Day 2*

I woke up somehow refreshed, feeling ready to take on the world! Was this program actually working? I couldn't wait to get back to that gray industrial park and meet up with all the other lunatics I had come to love in only twelve hours.

What they try to etch into your brain is this: You know what you know, you don't know what you don't know, and *apparently* what I knew in my past didn't happen the way I thought it did. Now I needed to know what had actually happened.

They talked a lot about preexisting notions; complaining being detrimental to your success; the difference between what really happens versus what your story is. I only remember any of this because I did exactly what they instructed us not to do—I took notes and wrote it all down and read it later. On the first day I had barely paid any attention, because it was just some stupid cult.

But now, I was fully *present*.

THE CULTIFICATION OF KRISTEN: *Day 3*

Mr. Namaste and I were now speaking the same language. And he was so proud of me!

My homework that day, on our only break, was to write a letter to someone toward whom you still felt resentment. I chose Lip Freckle Dude. (Remember Lip Freckle Dude? He was the heir to the flourishing carpet cleaning empire. Cheated on me on a cruise. Flip back a bit if you need to.)

I thought, once and for all, this act would free me from the guilt and shame I carried.

Here the letter is, in its entirety. Names have been changed to protect the innocent (or not so innocent).

Dear Lip Freckle Dude—

It's been years since we've spoken and I've recently completed a forum that has given me a new outlook on my life and ways to complete my past. In doing so, I want to share with you some things, and would like the chance to express how I have been inauthentic with you over the last 7 years.

I was unaware until this past weekend that I have been blaming you for so many things in my life that were never your fault. I remember writing you a letter about 2 years ago expressing my apologies for hurting you after the "cheating incident." I realize now that although I said those words, my intentions were not honest. I wrote that letter to make myself look good in your eyes. The intentions at the time were that if I apologized it would make me appear to be a good and honest person.

Starting now, I want to accept responsibility for the decisions that I made and apologize sincerely. I have had a complex in all of my relationships since you—it has been such that I've subconsciously been petrified of being alone, running from one relationship to the next, but also have had this incredible fear of commitment, and as a result it's been impossible for me to hold on to a successful relationship.

Over the years, I've been holding on to this thought that you made me dependent on you, and on men in general, because we dated for so long at such a young age. I also believed that I was held back from experiencing my first step into adulthood. I've been telling myself that your unfaithfulness has caused me to be untrusting, jealous, and insecure. I've been making you wrong for all of these things and none of them are true. I ran rackets on everyone close to me, meaning I made you wrong in order for me to be right—I win, you lose.

I regret all of those things because in reality, the stories I've created around those experiences were untrue—they were JUST the stories I created. I genuinely, from the bottom of my heart, apologize for making you wrong and blaming you and not accepting responsibility.

The truth is, you did have a great, positive effect on my life and who I am now! You aided in my INDEPENDENCE—by helping me become an adult. Seven years from meeting you, I still play the guitar and have this incredible relationship with music that I want to thank you for being a part of. The experiences we shared years ago have helped to make me a more diverse person and I'm extremely grateful.

You are down-to-earth and that has helped humble me. You were selfless and generous when you drove me around and let me borrow your car when I crashed mine—and I don't think I ever really thanked you for that in the way that I should have.

You introduced me to friends of yours who I still have amazing friendships with and without you that wouldn't have been possible. You took care of me when I was too young and immature to do so and gave up so much all because you cared. These are things I will carry with me for a lifetime and again, THANK YOU. All of those things I had been making you wrong for cost me our relationship, many friendships, respect for myself and from others.

The truth is, you have had an incredibly positive impact on my life and I really want to acknowledge you for that. You deserve all of the best that life has to offer you and I know you will continue to have a positive influence on others the way that you did on me. I have now created a possibility for my life and myself of being open, trusting, grateful, loving and forgiving. Again, thank you for that.

With all of these new possibilities in front of me I can also create a fulfilled life for myself and those that I love! I wish nothing but the best for you and for your family, with a future holding all of the great things life has to offer.

Love,

Kristen

I had become Ms. Namaste. I had found enlightenment. Then I received Lip Freckle Dude's response:

Dear Kristen—

What am I supposed to say to this? Im glad you could put me down to my friends to make yourself look good, thereby ruining many of my friendships. I forgave you a long time ago. Everyday we were together I had to forgive you just to look at you.

Why should I believe this attempt to reconcile is any different than before? I really cant understand why it is still so important for you to have my approval. I dont think about you, why do you still think about me?

It was a nice enough letter, I just dont understand why you would bother writing it after all this time. Maybe it was one of those letters you were supposed to write but never send. Just to make yourself feel better. Your [sic] good at that.

His reply was just cruel. OK, maybe I said my apology wasn't seeking a response, but subconsciously, I was. He didn't take an ounce of responsibility for what he had done, and honestly he was the one who should have been apologizing to me. He downplayed everything he ever did to me. I was hoping to mend the fence and move on without regret. I wanted to wash my hands of this past relationship. Maybe he was right—I shouldn't have sent it. He is the one who should have sent me the apology letter.

The cult made me feel like this situation was my fault, that my feelings were something I'd made up in my head.

The cult was a sham. I don't know how I fell for it.

Actually, I do. I was young, still trying to learn what being an adult even meant. I'd been skeptical, but in the classes I felt like maybe they were helping me navigate that. But at the end of the day, it was just a pyramid scheme—they didn't care about my self-growth, they were concerned with spreading the word and expanding their wallets. Thanks, Mr. Namaste.

He wanted me to be balanced and enlightened?

I decided I was OK with being a little crazy.

PART THREE

Kamikaze Kristen

My First Mactor

YOU MAY HAVE HEARD this one before: we "met at a party" . . . he was gorgeous but wore more accessories than I did. He had long flowing locks barely covered by his beanie, and wore a distressed tee with a button-down over it and a corduroy jacket over *that*—all monochromatic, of course. All this was topped with a non-scarf scarf-thing, a Dolce & Gabbana chain, and way too many bracelets. Fucking overkill . . . and I *loved it*.

He called me Guitar Girl. I was told he too played guitar, but it was more like played-*ish*. I would ultimately teach him. For our first date he asked me to go to a talent agency party. *This* is how you know you've met a Mactor—a model-slash-actor, a.k.a. 90 percent of men in Los Angeles. He is definitely also a bartender.

So, I met up with my Mactor at this talent agency party, solo. He was with a dude even better looking than him, plus four blonde chicks in stilettos. I strolled in wearing a band tee and chucks, and immediately thought I was being Punk'd. ("OK, Ashton! Come on out!") My insecurities multiplying by the millions, I took a deep breath and forced myself not to run, secretly daydreaming about how I might look with long blonde hair.

He squeezed my hand and flashed his perfect Mactor smile at me, and all was right with the world. He didn't want those SoCal glamour girls, he wanted *me*. At least for the night.

More than that was going to take some work.

I was all in from day one, but for him it was a slow build. Any straight Mactor has girls throwing themselves at him constantly. He could have anyone, but I knew we were meant to be. I just needed to show *him* that. I had to make a bold move.

I bought two tickets to a Cold War Kids show, knowing we both loved indie rock. I didn't actually ask him to go; I just told him I had two tickets. That's how I snagged him. A little manipulation never hurt anybody. He just needed a little nudge.

Dating a Mactor has its perks: hot male model friends, *never* waiting in line at nightclubs, and a plethora of hair care products. You never need to pack an overnight bag! My Mactor had everything I needed on him at all times, right down to the exact same shade of concealer I owned.

All these advantages come with their drawbacks, though. First and foremost is the narcissism. When you walk into a room with your Mactor, you think, *Are they looking at me, or at him?* Your Mactor always believes he's the main attraction, and he's not afraid to tell you so. He definitely had a more extensive beauty routine than I did, and somehow always had way too many beauty tips to share with me, completely unsolicited. Infamously, he regularly shaved his forehead. ("It's exfoliating," he said.) Once you start sharing jeans with your boyfriend, you start questioning your body image.

Was I his arm candy, or was he mine? He was so charismatic he could make me weak in the knees just by eyefucking me—but was he eyefucking everyone else, too?

We would get ready together at his vanity, and when he said "you're beautiful" I wondered if he was talking to me or to himself. His flat iron, oh, his *fucking* flat iron. It was his most prized possession. Would he ever look at me the way he looked at it?

Be forewarned, ladies: if you fall in love with a Mactor you will wake up every morning, look across the room, and see a dresser with a stack of head-shots, a *Breakthrough with Tony Robbins* DVD, and a human-sized jar of protein powder. On the wall above it will hang a giant photo of your Mactor in high school looking like an Abercrombie ad, daringly shirtless, his spiky boy band hair frosted with blond tips. You will stare at it for the rest of your life.

Glorified Roommates

THINGS ARE GOING WELL. Your relationship is ready for the next level. You want to move in together. Resist the urge. Do. Not. Do. It!

The truth is, it's all fun and games until you have to share a bathroom. At first it feels like you're playing house, but then it becomes really fucking real. You used to enjoy spending quality time together, but now time together means farting on the couch.

You used to watch porn together! Now it's just him up until four in the morning watching it by himself. If you get into an argument with him you can't take off and go home, because *you are home*, you *live together now*, and you *cannot escape*. Those little beard hair trimmings in the sink never go away, tiny reminders of your now-blackened soul.

The real kiss of death is when he tells you he "needs a boys' night." You used to slay boys' night! And date nights? Date nights are a waste. An exercise in futility. Beer is much cheaper at home.

What's the point in changing out of yoga pants? Do you really need to put makeup on around him anymore? You live together now. It all just sounds like a little too much effort.

And then there's *Valentine's Day*. Anyone with a brain will tell you this Hallmark holiday is *the worst*. Valentine's Day is the start to every big fight when you're "just" living with someone. The expectation is never met. The expectation is too high. *Are we moving to the next level? What are we even doing here? Are we going to* just *live together forever? Did you buy those carnations on the off ramp at Forest Lawn Drive?*

My first live-in boyfriend *loovveedddd* online poker. To be fair, once things started to cool off between us he loved anything that took his attention away from me: video games, his trumpet, even alien shows on the Discovery Channel. Online poker, though, was top choice.

One night as he sat on our couch playing online poker for the eighth day in a row I put my foot down. Enough was enough. I got on my knees and just *went* for it. He was about to get the best blowjob of his life. And he pushed me away like a leper.

I was wearing fucking *lingerie!* I was twenty-six, hot, skinny, and drop-dead gorgeous. He would rather get two-pair, aces high, than a BJ from his model girlfriend.

To make matters worse, his guy friends were always over at our apartment. They had their own keys, slept on our couch, ate all of our food, and sided with him any time we were in a fight. They loved to leave ridiculous, gross porn from weird magazines all over the apartment. I would find it under my pillow, on the toilet seat, and inside every cabinet. Not just a one-time prank, but an endless parade of gonzo porn, 365 days a year.

Looking back, I should have known it was time to move out when I started slamming the microwave door. I was very gentle with appliances prior to living with this man! He would always say I acted irrational, I was overly emotional, and I acted like a psycho. But when you're living with someone like him, someone who had decided I didn't matter anymore, I had to get noticed *somehow.*

Unfortunately, I didn't trust my intuition, and lived with him for Four. More. Long. Years.

You? You should get out now.

16

Sin City Slipup

IF THERE'S EVEN A HINT that there are cracks in your relationship, do *not* let your boyfriend go to Vegas—even if it's for work. No, *especially* if it's for work. The working girls in the hotel casinos can smell a man that's alone on a "business trip" a mile away. I'm not saying this girl was necessarily a sex worker, but her name definitely sounded like "her first pet's name" combined with "name of the street she grew up on."

I was at home in Los Angeles, minding my own business, when I was tagged in a suspicious tweet. This particular tweet was of great interest to me, as it featured a photo of a girl, wearing my boyfriend's shirt, in a hotel room in Vegas. The same hotel I knew he was staying at that weekend. The hunt was on and it only took me 2.5 seconds. This was child's play. Long before my boyfriend returned from his weekend of transgression I had already tracked down Vegas Girl. All I had to do was search our shared phone bill. I called every single phone number with a Vegas area code until I got the girl's voicemail. I cross referenced her name, found her real social media accounts, and direct messaged her. She knew she was caught and confirmed he cheated.

All that was left to do was wait for him to get home.

As soon as he walked through the front door, I confronted him, fully expecting him to deny it, but he shocked me by *admitting the truth*. He had cheated, I caught him, and he copped to it. Noble, sure, but *I wasn't ready for that*. If he had just lied to me, it would have been easier for me to deny it to myself, to explain it away, and to tell all our friends nothing had happened. Fuck.

So obviously, there are a few options available to you when you're living with someone and get cheated on:

1. Pack a bag and bolt to your girlfriend's house.
2. Throw his shit out and change the locks.
3. Lock yourself in your bathroom with headphones and a bottle of Jack Daniel's, plotting your revenge.

OR

4. Forgive him immediately because he was honest with you, and go out with your friends.

I should have chosen option one or two, but I went for an unhealthy mixture of three and four. We'd been together for four years! I wasn't going to give up on us so easily.

Plus . . . he didn't want to break up with me. He wanted me to do the dirty work and break up with *him*.

Guys can be cowards; they're lazy about confrontation. It was easier for my boyfriend to stay with me in our low-rent apartment than to leave. We shared a phone bill and a DVR box—our lives were intertwined. He was over me, over us, but was too much of a coward to end it.

The only thing left to do in a situation like this is, naturally, to completely misplace the blame and take your anger and aggression out on the other woman. Luckily, I had friends that would happily go down that road with me.

I wasn't proud of myself for coming for her. It was five minutes of satisfaction followed by hours of self-reflection. But I was angry, and I felt disrespected. I was even less proud of myself once I finally got in real contact with her and heard her side of the story: he'd told her he was single, that we were broken up.

I could no longer lie to myself—this was 100 percent his fault. His excuse was that it only happened because "we were going through a rough patch." The idea that we were past that patch gave me a false sense of hope. In hindsight, the relationship was already over. I knew it, he knew it, everyone knew it. But we stayed together because it was easier—and because I didn't want to give up.

I don't know if "people cheat in Vegas" is true for everybody, but it's a cliché for a reason. What happens in Vegas doesn't always stay in Vegas.

To Catch a Cheater

Don't just stalk him . . . Investigate.

🦋 GOOOOOOOOOGLE. Him

94 percent of the male population is Googleable. Do it. You should have done this on day one, honey. Do you find his profile on dating sites? Probably. If a guy doesn't have *any* sort of social media footprint, *run*. That's not a private person, that's a liar who knows he can't keep his lies straight online.

🦋 Dating Sites

Get a burner number, sign up for Tinder with a fake photo, and right swipe away in the one-mile radius around where he lives. Wait for *it's a match*.

🦋 Search History

This is a treasure trove of information. You will definitely not like what you see, cheater or not. Guys are disgusting.

Multiple Email Addresses

He says he uses them to avoid spam. That is not why he uses them. He is using them to log on to hookup sites and find other women to bang in the neighborhood.

Password Reset and Security Questions

Once you're in, change everything so he can't get it back. *Write it all down.* How much would it suck to do all of this hard investigative work just to forget what you'd chosen later?

Credit Card Statements, Phone Bills, Etc.

Always the easiest way to catch a cheater. Black and white, baby. He'll probably still deny it and say a burglar stole his credit card and phone, bought that lingerie that he didn't give you, and placed all those calls to some random girl's phone at booty call hours. Sure.

Passcode Phone Unlock

If you weren't smart enough to snatch his phone at one point early in your relationship and set up facial recognition with your own face, you'll have to settle for holding his phone at the perfect angle, under the perfect light, to figure out his numeric passcode from the fingerprints on his screen. Good luck.

🦋 Dirty Laundry

Like *legit* dirty laundry. Ew, I know. But you can find all kinds of incriminating things in the pockets of a cheater's pants.

🦋 Chat Rooms

Maybe it's nothing sexual and he just likes gaming chat rooms. If this is the case, run anyway.

I Lied

THIS IS THE HARDEST chapter to write, because I've spent years consciously repressing all details, memories, and feelings that I have about this major fuckup. You likely know some of this story already, but I'll try to give you the rest.

I was in my late twenties, and my five-year relationship had been through more turmoil than Britney and Kevin Federline managed in that one season of *Chaotic* on UPN. I was totally codependent, and the two of us lived in a world of denial and barely there contentment. I was younger than I realized, secretly depressed, and on a downward spiral of bad decision-making: drinking way too much, partying way too much, and constantly engaging in toxic fights with my boyfriend. I was getting zero attention from him, and as much as we loved each other—and we really did—by that point we also couldn't stand each other.

But neither of us was ever going to leave. I knew in the back of my mind that we were done, I just didn't want to believe it. He was all I knew. He was my best friend, my lifeline. I was absolutely terrified that if we broke up, no one would ever love me again.

Then came the night that changed the course of my life, forever.

It was a night like any other, my boyfriend and I—and his friends—watching TV at our house, drinking and hanging out. And by "drinking and hanging out" I mean face-chugging Four Loko. To be honest, I don't remember much. I know it happened. I know *he* wasn't my boyfriend. I know we were both drunk, but also that we made a mutual, consensual decision. I'm still not sure how it could have happened, but it did. I slept with my boyfriend's best friend, who not too long before this used to date *my* former best friend.

I decided, right afterward, that this would be something I would never think about ever, ever, *ever* again. Nothing I would ever speak aloud. A blip in the radar . . . and I willed it gone. Out of my mind for good, like it had never happened.

The next time I saw the guy was at Chardonnay Monday—a weekly routine with some friends of mine, a group hang without my boyfriend. It was just a girls' night that this guy had somehow become part of, where we would talk ad nauseum and console him about the fallout of his relationship with his ex, our former friend. When he showed up there and it felt normal, I thought maybe nothing had changed. He didn't mention it, or look at me any differently. We were still the best of platonic friends. Maybe it *didn't* happen? Maybe I'd dreamed it.

But then it happened again.

The gory details: My boyfriend and I got into another one of our knock-down, drag-out arguments, and my boyfriend *called* that same friend to come pick me up and take me someplace else. Wasted. We were wasted, again. We were wasted a lot back then.

Looking back, I just wanted attention and affection, and it didn't matter anymore from whom or from where. I'd barely hugged my boyfriend, let alone had sex with him, in months. I was longing to feel desired, to know that I was still worth something. My self-love tank was entirely depleted, and I hated every minute of it. Hooking up with *this guy* again was the ultimate self-sabotage, which is something I was really good at.

It wasn't planned. It wasn't purposeful. But it *was* selfish. But I was lonely and for some reason I felt safe and familiar with him and all my morals went out the window. My total lack of self-esteem, plus a lot of alcohol, made it feel totally reasonable to commit the ultimate relationship crime. Twice.

Somehow, I thought I could bury this and take it to my grave. I should have known better. As soon as one person found out— and, of course, someone did—word hit the street and I reacted exactly as you would expect: I lied. Knowing a confession would destroy my life, I came up with a plan to cover my tracks.

I knew my boyfriend well enough to know that at any hint of impropriety, he would snatch my phone and text his friend, pretending to be me. We were both actors, after all. I told the friend that I would *never* text him about this situation, and if any text came from my phone about having sex with him, it was *not me!*

I tested him a few times, texting him out of the blue about it, and each time he passed with flying colors. This was going to work. I could keep on lying and denying, and the truth would never come out. For a while, it worked.

After almost a year of being free and clear, many things had changed: the guy's ex-girlfriend and I were BFFs again, much to my relief, but he was also desperately trying to get her back. I was dealing with a scandal surrounding my *boyfriend* cheating, all the while still covering up my own indiscretions. And meanwhile, my hometown of Detroit had filed for bankruptcy. Let's just say the summer was not looking up.

To top it all off, the guy secretly confessed to everyone else behind my back.

I still kept my lie going for as long as I could, because I was in too deep now. Until the confrontation. Until the bitch slap heard around the world.

In that moment I became evil, and the man I cheated with was absolved. Sure, everyone knew he was an "asshole"—but they expected this kind of behavior from him, from men, so somehow, he drifted through the whole thing fairly unscathed.

I still thought I could get out of it, because this guy was a known liar. So, I lied and lied until I physically couldn't bear it anymore. It ate at me until I finally came clean and admitted that he was telling the truth. It was my true rock bottom.

To reopen these wounds and share this with you is really hard because, like I said, I've repressed this. After years of apologies I was eventually, graciously, forgiven by the people I wronged, but I have tried to never speak of it again. I've never told my side because I was so embarrassed, and so disappointed in myself, that I didn't feel I was allowed to have feelings.

What frustrates me to this day is that the guy was never held equally to blame. No one knew better than him how toxic my relationship was. To me, back then, those brief moments of infidelity with him gave me a false sense of self-worth, a feeling of being desired that kept me from crawling deeper into my dark hole of self-loathing. I was humiliated. I knew it was wrong, but so did he. Years later this is still held against me, my Scarlet Letter, while the world has allowed him to let it go.

People always ask if I did all this on purpose, subconsciously, to give me and my boyfriend a real reason to finally break up. I don't know if that's true, but I do know what I did, and I take full responsibility for it: I slept with my boyfriend's best friend, who was *my* best friend's recent ex. Twice.

The Hail Mary

IN FOOTBALL AND IN LIFE, a Hail Mary is a last-ditch effort in desperation, with only a tiny chance of success.

Finding out that my ex—the one I thought I *might* still be in love with—had cheated on his new girlfriend was like waking up to a shitload of presents on Christmas morning.

I wasn't entirely sure I wanted him back, but I certainly didn't want *them* together. He had left me for her, and now he had cheated on her. I just *knew* once his new girlfriend heard this information, they would be done. Vengeance would be mine. I felt vindicated that now, he had done this *again* to someone else. The someone else he left me for. Now she would know what it felt like to be cheated on by him. After her dismissiveness of my feelings and our breakup, it was time for her to become paranoid and mistrustful of him. She would finally see that I wasn't the crazy one after all.

And then maybe we'd move back in together? Maybe we could work on things that had gotten out of control? Maybe that was all just a bad patch we had to get past. After all, I *was* still getting mail at our old apartment. I hadn't even changed my forwarding address.

Except his new girlfriend didn't believe the rumor. She trusted him! He would *never* cheat on her.

Really, bitch?

I was still in pain and feeling vengeful and attached five months after our breakup, so, as always, I took matters into my own hands. It only took me a hot minute to find this girl he'd allegedly cheated with, Miami Girl, on Instagram. (Oh, social media, you make things way too easy.) I sent her a DM, simply asking if the rumor was true, and she wrote me back immediately *demanding* to be heard.

I had unearthed the missing link. I couldn't possibly sit on this information: not only had he cheated, Miami Girl said he was still in love with me! Yeah, she gave me a few unnecessary details about their sexcapade that I really didn't need to know. But more important, she claimed that he kept talking about *me*, about our failed relationship, and about how much he missed me. She knew details about our relationship that no one but him would know. There was no way she was lying. This was music to my ears.

In a stroke of luck she happened to be coming to L.A. soon to visit family. In my plot to ruin my ex's new relationship, I had to take this opportunity when it presented itself. We made plans to meet up at a discreet location (Canter's, Fairfax Avenue). The last thing I wanted to do was bond over brunch with some girl who had a one-night stand with my ex-boyfriend, but she needed my help! She wanted to *confront* him.

Let me be clear: I appreciated the sentiment, as I would have done the exact same thing to a man who called me a liar. I would want to confront him face to face.

We concocted our diabolical plan and decided it would happen that night. I was sweating, my stomach in knots, so I slammed an entire bottle of sauvignon blanc in the hour we were there. I needed to be stress-free for the ultimate ambush that was about to go down.

The thing is, back then we all worked at a restaurant together: me, my ex, and his new girlfriend. Maybe you've heard of it—SUR? Sexy Unique Restaurant?

I wasn't scheduled to work that day, but I knew my ex and his girlfriend would be working behind the bar together. My plan: a friend and I would get there first, sit front row, and watch as Miami Girl walked in and confronted him. I *needed* to witness this all go down.

SUR

Sexy. Unique. Restaurant. This bothers me. That isn't why the restaurant was originally named SUR back when I started working there. Sur means "South" in Spanish and "On" in French, which are co-owner couple Guillermo and Nathalie's native languages. *Somehow,* years later, it acquired this corny acronym.

My friend and I were dressed to the nines. I borrowed her only designer dress, because *she* couldn't wear it, *I* needed to wear it. I looked fantastic—like, fake lashes, the whole shebang. Basically, I was giving my ex a moment to really check me out without my SURver dress on. He and his new girlfriend were behind the bar, watching my every move as I sat there in my Versace. It was working.

My heart pounded in anticipation. I knew it was about to happen. Miami Girl texted me that she had arrived. *This was it!* I was ready for him to be caught, for his big breakup with the new girl to happen.

Would he be mad at me for a minute? Yeah, sure. But at some point, he would forgive me. He still loved me. We'd been in worse fights.

Miami Girl sashayed up to the bar, calm as could be, and *ordered a fucking cosmo*. The balls this bish had! Their quick confrontation happened in a flash: "We had sex!" "No, we didn't!" "Yes, we did!" "No, we didn't!"

I was waiting for his new girlfriend to jump in and tear his head off, but instead . . . she grabbed his arm and they bolted. They both left the restaurant in a sprint.

It wasn't going to end that easily. *Not on my watch.*

I ran into the back-alley parking lot after them, only to watch as they jumped into a car and sped off *together*! Nightmare.

Unfortunately, it wasn't over for me just yet. Not only did they not break up (they are still together now!) but I got fired from my job for causing a stir. *Whatever.* Suck a dick.

Robbing the Cradle

THERE'S A RITE OF PASSAGE for every woman in her sexual prime, and that's dating a younger guy. Forget fighting about taking out the trash, honey-do lists, and whose turn it is to do the dishes—when you're dating a younger guy, you tend to cut him some slack. You don't place all the usual requirements on him that you normally would, because you remember what it was like being his age. You make more allowances. (Sometimes you *give* him an allowance.) You don't judge him for being broke, having no direction, failing to keep a job, living in a makeshift room in someone else's living room, or still living with his parents.

The only thing that matters is: he *adores* you. He worships the ground you walk on. He thinks you're the bee's knees, the best thing that's ever happened to him. And you, being the worldly cougar (or puma), will teach him the ways of the world.

This was a very appealing proposition for me because I had just turned thirty and my tumultuous relationship of nearly six years had suddenly ended with a giant, resounding *thud*.

My younger guy weaseled his way into my life by acting as if he was the only person who really had my back. My ex had already moved on, so why shouldn't I at least *act* like I had moved on? This kid was the perfect mirage. Surely no one would ever see through my thinly veiled attempt to prove to everyone that I was completely over my ex.

A twenty-one-year-old was in love with *me*. That's right, I still got it! Stella fully had her groove back.

At first, it was almost like being in a high school relationship again. Sex *all the time*. No place was off-limits. No time was off-limits. We were running around like nymphomaniacs without a care in the world. No one would ever believe just how much ridiculous fun we were having together. All he wanted to do was impress me—not with money (he didn't have any), but with his wild adventures and willingness to do whatever I wanted (I was paying anyway).

I get the appeal of dating an older chick. We are confident, know what we want, know how to get it, and, rumor has it, we're at our sexual prime. When the young guy gets emotional, we can be calm.

One night he picked me up from work (in my car, because he didn't have one) and drove me to the beach at midnight with champagne (possibly Vanderpump Rosé) and strawberries (he probably stole these from a street vendor). We sat on the beach under the stars talking about philosophy (people we hated at SUR) and literature (*Family Guy* memes on his phone).

It's amazing looking back now in hindsight how I glamorized these events in the moment.

Just try to have a night out with your friends with your newly minted Cradle Rob tagging along. Mine was loud, ill-mannered, and couldn't have a glass of wine without it turning into World War III.

All my new guy wanted to do was party. Sure, going to a club made me feel young for a minute, but *only* for a minute. He would throw tantrums if I didn't want to party. He would borrow my car and return it looking like it had been a stunt car on the set of *Twister*.

He had less relationship baggage than an older guy, but no coping skills; when life's problems arrived at his door, it was like I was his mom, not his equal. And I *really* did not want to turn into *this* guy's mom.

He couldn't figure out how to do anything, and we couldn't even fight about washing dishes because hell would freeze over before he'd sponge anything but his balls. And the "not a care in the world" attitude became unbearable. Only a guy that age can turn being present into a bad thing. They're too in the moment—they don't think about repercussions. They're not thinking about tomorrow, let alone a five-year plan.

My brother is one year younger than me, so I've always considered anyone younger than him a child. I was in fourth grade when my Cradle Rob was born. He was an exception for which I'd broken my rule. I could have *babysat* him when I was his age, and in the end that's exactly what I ended up doing. Babysitting a morally, emotionally, and literally bankrupt ankle-biter.

It has an allure, a mystique to it, but dating a younger guy is not all it's cracked up to be. Mostly it's just annoying. Does he think it's cute that he doesn't have a car? That he plays video games all day? That he drinks like he's never seen Nicolas Cage in *Leaving Las Vegas*? (Oh my God; he was three years old when *Leaving Las Vegas* came out.)

This was supposed to be fun. It wasn't. But with everything that was toxic in my life at the time, I was ready to double down and *really* drive this speeding, out-of-control relationship straight into the ditch.

Ubergate

I WAS AT A FRIEND'S birthday party during the tail end of a horrific relationship. My boyfriend was chugging Fireball straight out of the bottle and trashed to the point where he was too much for me to handle. I left the party, unconcerned with his partying plan for the rest of the night. He was a big boy now, and he could figure out how to get home.

The next day, he wasn't answering his phone. When I hadn't heard from him all day I called Birthday Girl to see if she knew his whereabouts or how he had gotten home. She said she put him in an Uber from the hotel party with another girlfriend of ours who lived near him.

Birthday Girl forwarded me the Uber receipt—which we then noticed went from my boyfriend's house straight to Burbank, twelve miles and thirty minutes away. That meant what should have been a six-dollar Uber was in fact a thirty-dollar Uber, with no rhyme or reason as to why one or both of them went to another location.

Our first assumption—we trusted this girl!—was that she was probably hooking up with someone in Burbank. Or maybe they'd gone to another party together?

I made Birthday Girl contact Uber immediately, only to find out that they were actually only dropped off at my boyfriend's address. The Uber driver had forgotten to turn off his meter as he moved on to pick up someone new in Burbank.

Motherfucker.

Being me, I didn't call my boyfriend out right away. Instead, Detective Doute got to work. Back at my apartment, he had left his laptop unlocked with his password off and his email wide open. Men make this *so* easy. I searched his email for "Uber" and when I didn't get the receipt I wanted, I searched the Trash folder. *Bingo.* An Uber receipt from his address to the girl's address at 7:00 AM. Once again, a guy had forgotten to empty his trash.

Later that day, I asked him to meet me for lunch. He was hungover, vulnerable, and completely clueless. I simply asked how his night had gone after I left. He admitted that after the party, an Uber had picked them up together, but he claimed it dropped him off first, then took the girl home. I showed him the evidence, and he knew he was caught. This wasn't my first Ubergate.

Passwords on iTunes are Steve Jobs's gift that keeps on giving. See, Apple passwords are all connected. The passwords to your iTunes, your iCloud, and your iPhone tracker are exactly the same. Catch your shady boyfriend in a good mood when you two are jamming to some music together, and take action.

"Honey, I wanted to download some music on your iTunes and I can't download them to the library! What's your login again?"

You can now track his every dishonest move.

When this guy and I finally broke up, I used his login for one last hurrah. When you get into "Find My Phone," notice that little button that says "Erase"? I erased everything on his iPad. Immature? Sure. Satisfying? *Damn right.*

Look, I could have erased his desktop computer. I could have erased his phone. After all, his phone was the accessory that aided him in years of sending selfies and flirty quips to other women! I chose to leave myself with at least one shot glass full of dignity—I only took revenge on the iPad. *And it felt good.*

Bye-bye, baby.

My Darkest Hour

ABUSE COMES IN MANY different forms. It's hard to talk about it. I never thought it would happen to me, I denied it when it did, and I downplayed it when somebody else found out.

This particular guy started out as a fun rebound fling masked as a relationship. It didn't end up that way, unfortunately. His abusive behavior crept in slowly at first, with name-calling and hypercriticism every other day. I thought I could handle those things. I'm a tough girl with pretty healthy self-esteem when I'm at my best, so I would just forgive him every time he apologized for his mean and insulting outbursts. But then every other day turned into every day.

I was confused. If *any* of my friends had been in this situation I would've kicked that guy's ass and told my friend they weren't putting up with that bullshit anymore. Somehow, I wasn't applying that same standard to my own relationship.

The thing is, I didn't anticipate how this guy could really mess with my self-esteem so steadily, so methodically, that I didn't realize the switch had happened until it was too late. By the time he had broken me down, I was fully ready to let it get to the next level. He was jealous and possessive. He put me down in public and blamed me for all his problems.

And then it escalated. Broken furniture, shattered picture frames and mirrors, doors slamming, and holes punched in my walls. Once that line had been crossed, it was only a matter of time before he put his hands on *me*: shoving, pushing, and physical restraint.

Somehow, he could do all of these things and still manipulate me into staying with him. Once he'd calmed down he would apologize, always so contrite, always promising it would never happen again. Until it happened again and again and again.

He was really good at making me feel guilty and better at making me feel like I deserved it.

He knew some stories of my "crazy past" and used them against me in any way he could. He told me no one would ever love me or be with me if I left him, and that I'd be alone forever. I believed him.

There were so many times I wanted out and thought I had the strength to leave for good. His apologies and cries for help always roped me back in. He would tell me how depressed he was and beg for my forgiveness. *How can I leave someone who needs real help?* He had made me feel so responsible for his mental health that I asked myself this question over and over again.

Not many people knew the truth of what was going on, because I felt humiliated that I kept going back to him. How could I tell the truth but stay with him anyway? So I would downplay our fights and shrug off the many times he would publicly embarrass me.

Eventually the friends of mine who did witness the abuse refused to be near him anymore and said that if I stayed with him, they would cut me out too. He mostly did everything behind closed doors, so it was my word against his. Sometimes he would remember what he'd done, and sometimes he claimed he didn't, but either way he always called me a liar.

He wasn't just a prick. He was cruel. He took every insecurity I'd ever confided in him and shoved them down my throat. He liked to dig deep, to go for the jugular.

After one of the worst nights, I broke up with him again. This time, I did it calmly, because I was afraid I would work him back up. I asked for space and expressed that I wasn't ready to talk to him just then. He responded, "You are not single, so don't go thinking you are. You better not be telling people we are not together, because it's not true." I felt trapped.

His family always backed him up and defended him, even when I told them I was afraid to be alone with him. *He has a lot on his plate. He isn't just some guy. He's anxious. You know he loves you.* There was nothing they wouldn't excuse.

Thankfully, somehow I finally hit that breaking point. I realized I'd lost all sense of self-worth, and I knew that if I truly wanted to rebuild my life he couldn't be a part of it. My friends slowly started coming back around when they believed this time it was for real, and promised me they would stick by me if I stuck to my guns. So I did.

I forced myself to remember that this guy started as a rebound, was someone I'd gone to for comfort, and that this wasn't a real, loving relationship. Because love doesn't look like that. It can't.

It was not my fault. I deserved better. And if you are in a situation like the one I'm describing, you deserve better too.

Blind Date

DATING APPS ARE AWKWARD, because it feels like you have only a nano-second to decide how to present yourself to the world as a bad-ass hot prospect. It's stressful! How many photos do you add? What *kind* of photos do you add? Do you bedazzle your sad, single persona with a three-sentence bio? Talk about your dogs, with a hint of sarcasm? Do you go full-on facetious, praying these dudes get your sometimes obscure sense of humor? Or should the whole thing be well thought out and intricate, like my old MySpace manifestos?

I had never been on a dating app before, but one of my friends dared me to try out Bumble while we were driving to a Third Eye Blind concert. It was new at the time, and the gimmick was that the women had control; if you and a guy both swiped for each other, only the girl could make the first move. I chose one photo—a new black and white headshot—only I accidentally uploaded it twice. My profile had only my age, sex, and location. My go-to opening line: "Hey, what's up?"

I had zero game.

He was my first right swipe, and the only guy from the app I ever gave my number to. We started texting almost immediately, lightly making plans for an "adult bev" on his side of town. I was swooning over his photos, his demeanor, and our banter. Everything felt so natural! I blushingly bragged about him to one of my best friends, thinking how crazy it would be to go on a date with someone I'd never actually met. To be honest, I'd never really been on a proper *date* with someone new.

And, of course, she knew him. I swear L.A. is the smallest world in the largest city in the country.

Apparently, he'd had a one-night stand with our *other* best friend a decade prior, but because that friend was engaged at this point, I wouldn't be breaking girl code. He was still fair game. Thank God.

The fact that my friends knew him actually made me feel safer; I didn't have to worry about being chopped into little pieces in some random Venice Beach alleyway at the end of our date. It turned out I knew a lot of his friends, too. It was kind of a picture-perfect scenario.

We planned our date for the very next day on the Westside, near where he lived. I chose to drive, *just in case*, and met him at the Misfit in Santa Monica for dinner and drinks. To this day, it was the best date I've ever been on. It didn't take long to snag my first kiss from him, and our eyes were locked the entire night—except for when I felt a little too comfortable and decided I should Periscope a portion of the date. (Periscope is Twitter's version of Instagram Live. Listen, I was excited and happy and just wanted to be ME!)

We roamed around to a couple other spots and decided to call it a night. I didn't want to leave him, but I didn't want to seem desperate or clingy either. He walked me back to the parking garage where we were both parked . . . and my car was nowhere to be seen.

What the hell? I had literally taken photos of not only the parking garage address but a 360-degree view of exactly where my car was! We then realized, at 12:35 AM, that I had accidentally parked my car in the *private* garage next door, which had closed at midnight. Fuck my life.

Yet he was unfazed by my mistake! He was so calm, so cool and collected. He said it was no big deal and he could drive us to his apartment—he would sleep on the couch and I could have his bed. My God, he was so refined. As he held the door open for me into his place, I walked into a gorgeous Venice bachelor pad—with no couch. So instead we made out like teenagers and then I had sex with him in his kitchen. You only live once.

It was a magical night, and we woke up the next morning basically in love. I didn't want to appear too eager, so we spent the next few weeks dating occasionally, reintroducing each other to our respective friend groups, and going on summer adventures. We hit up concerts, volleyball tournaments, and even a turtle race. This was the *fun* I'd been craving in a relationship for years.

We said "I love you" twenty-five days later at the Petit Ermitage hotel, at a friend's Sunday Funday pool party.

For the next three years we spent our anniversary there every August 23.

Two and a half months after our first date, I invited him to come to New York City with me for the wedding of one of my oldest friends. I was so proud to be on his arm, and I couldn't wait to stroll around Central Park together. It was real life *Serendipity*. Fate had brought us together, and our first vacation was flawless.

Then, just days after returning to Los Angeles, we went to a wine bar with his friends and the night ended in tragedy. Not because we had our first fight or anything like that. No, it was because my baby-giraffe-on-ice-skates self tripped getting out of the Uber and broke my face. I broke my orbital socket in three places. I looked like a nightmare. My Bumble Boy was forced to either flee the relationship or straight away jump into husband/caretaker mode with his new girlfriend. Great guy that he was, he chose the latter.

I spent the next two weeks holed up in his apartment, half-blind and swollen in his bed, while he took time off from his job to care for me. After my facial reconstruction surgery, Bumble Boy spent all three nights in the hospital with me, sleeping on a chair and sometimes in my bed. He then took on the responsibility of caring for me in those first difficult weeks afterward, when I was healing. He was the picture of perfection and compassion. I knew it was time to move in together, because if he had proposed right then, we would be married right now.

After everything I'd been through in my last several relationships, I decided I wasn't going to waste any time. I couldn't let the past hold me back. This was my person. They say when you know, you know—and I *knew*. I didn't care if people said I was crazy again, this time because I'd jumped in so fast. This man was my soulmate.

He moved into my apartment while we looked for a bigger place, our first, together as a couple. It was going so well that a week later, when he was visiting family in Georgia for Thanksgiving, I decided we should have a dog together. How better to find out what kind of father he would be? So, by month four, we were a full-on family, complete with puppy.

Dating Profiles 101

These tips are for guys hoping to meet girls on the apps.

🦋 **DON'T** brandish a gun in your profile picture. Nobody will want to date you. *Nobody*. Unless she's also brandishing a gun in hers, in which case I wish you two the best of luck.

🦋 **DON'T** have multiple car selfies or multiple gym selfies (or, really, *any* gym selfies).

🦋 **DON'T** have other women in your photo, unless it's your mom.

🦋 **DON'T** have other guys in your photo, either, forcing us to try to figure out which one is you. Nobody has the time or patience for that.

🦋 And, for the love of God, if you want anyone to swipe right, **DON'T** wear sunglasses in *every single picture*.

🦋 **DON'T** use a professional headshot. I realize I told you that I did this. It was wrong. I know that now.

🦋 **DON'T** use an old high school photo. We will know when we meet you in person and see that you are now bald.

🦋 **DON'T** say this is your first time. We know it's a lie.

🦋 **DON'T** be a buzzkill. We don't want to hear you whine about your ex or your mean boss. And please, there's a thing called spellcheck. Use it.

🦋 **NO POLITICS WHATSOEVER.** You can fight about that on the date.

🦋 **NO CAT PHOTOS.** Dogs all day, every day.

🦋 **NO MOTTOS.** This includes Teamwork Makes the Dream Work, No Pain / No Gain, It's Just the Way the Cookie Crumbles, Seize the Day, YOLO, FOMO, JOMO, or any other OLO or OMO.

If you can't play by these rules, I hear Facebook is starting a Dating page, so go there. I'm sure they allow everything.

The Honeymoon Phase

WHEN YOU'RE IN THE honeymoon phase you never realize or admit to yourself that it's happening. In your mind, this really *is* perhaps the greatest love of all time, and no other couple on the planet has ever experienced such pure bliss as the two of you.

This period of limited euphoria involves speaking to each other in baby voices, giving each other pet names, and laughing at each other's *adorable* shortcomings. You sit on the same side of the table at restaurants, wish you had thirteen hands so you could have more hands touching each other at the same time, and know exactly what the other person is thinking just by gazing into each other's eyes. Another thing you tend to do during these rose-colored early months is judge everyone else's relationships. Not only are you now a relationship *expert*, your finger-wagging advice to others is often laughable and patronizing.

When Bumble Boy and I were in our honeymoon phase, I was convinced I had finally found my one and only. Everything was going to be perfect. I bought a fake engagement ring in the style I wanted, just to take it for a test drive before I got the real thing! I was already planning our springtime, boho, hipster-chic wedding. We would have a minimum of ten in our bridal party and the bridesmaids *could* each wear a differently colored bridesmaid dress *as long as* it was mauve, cream, and/or gold, the color scheme I had shared with him on a Pinterest board. We would be married at sunset, and fireworks would fly as we walked down the aisle as Man and Wife. My life was coming together, just as I had fantasized so many times as a little girl.

One advantage of being in the throes of the honeymoon delusion was having extra time to help my friends! Their relationships, I thought, were clearly inadequate compared to mine. With my own life settled, I was now free to interject myself as deeply and messily as I liked into all their wobbly relationships. It was time to fix things! I was helping.

Even engaged couples, at their shared bachelor/bachelorette party, were not off-limits.

It was our first day in New Orleans for the occasion, and my engaged best friends couldn't even make it through the night without winding up in an argument. I knew it wasn't really about the little jabs and complaints; there was something bigger looming over them. It was a cheating rumor. He denied it, but she clearly didn't believe him. If *they* weren't going to talk about it, I was going to find a way to *make* them talk about it. I didn't want them walking down the aisle without getting to the bottom of it.

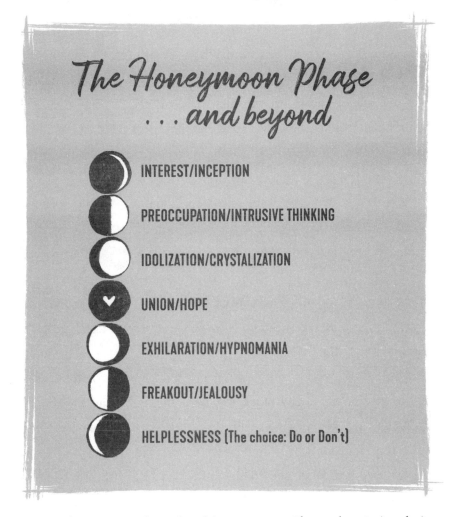

The Honeymoon Phase
. . . and beyond

INTEREST/INCEPTION

PREOCCUPATION/INTRUSIVE THINKING

IDOLIZATION/CRYSTALIZATION

UNION/HOPE

EXHILARATION/HYPNOMANIA

FREAKOUT/JEALOUSY

HELPLESSNESS (The choice: Do or Don't)

At the time, I thought this was my gift to them! As their bridesmaid, and as the person who introduced them in the first place all those years ago, it felt like my *duty*. Now that I was in a healthy relationship of my own, with the most honest man I'd ever dated, I couldn't imagine something like this hanging over our heads. I believed I had achieved a heightened sense of awareness, an enlightenment about how relationships should be. If only my friends could communicate the way Bumble Boy and I did!

We talked about everything, and always talked everything through. *We* never fought, and when we disagreed we always reached a compromise. As the new and improved Kristen, the Kristen who'd found all the answers, my role going forward clearly would be to help everyone else navigate the flaws in their relationships. If there was an elephant in the room, I would bring it up. Nobody else was going to do it.

Just to set the scene here, my friend's fiancé and his buddies went out dressed in drag for his bachelor party. On a normal bachelor's night out on the town, you would expect fellas to get pretty lit. Now imagine *just* how drunk some straight guys partying in drag were by the end of the night. Lipstick smudged, dresses a bit tattered—perfect time for a confrontation, right? It made sense at the time.

I pulled the groom-to-be away from his friends, asked him for a one-on-one chat, and stuck my nose in his business where it didn't belong. Needless to say, it didn't go well. He listened for a solid four seconds before he became infuriated and dipped out. I followed him through the hotel lobby, pleading with him to hear me out—because I'd been in bad relationships, and now I knew better!

He stomped to the elevator, shouting over and over at me to just *stay out of it*.

Look, it was none of my business, but it had come from a place of love and concern. And maybe a little arrogance, because that honeymoon phase really hits you hard.

You'd think I would've learned my lesson, but I did this more than once.

Another time, another one of my best friends was fighting with her boyfriend. She kept telling me she wanted to go back to her hometown in Kentucky to escape for a while, and I was nervous that if she went off to Kentucky, she might never come back. I refused to let this man's antics have that deep of an effect on her psyche.

All she kept saying was that she wanted her mom—so I brought her mom to her. I bought her mom a ticket to Los Angeles.

No, it's not common to fly in a friend's mom in an effort to break up a relationship, but I did because I thought I knew what was best for her. I get how it looks. *Meddlesome* would be a kind word. But this is what can happen when you're still in the honeymoon phase. I had a false idea of what a *real* relationship looked like. My head was still in the clouds, and it made me self-righteous.

Looking back, Bumble Boy and I had our own set of issues. Ultimately, I did realize we might not have the greatest love of all time. Other couples on the planet had experienced pure bliss like the two of us did in those first few months, that first year.

Behind closed doors, here was the truth: at the first indication of a disagreement, I would regress back to every argument I ever had in my past, dysfunctional relationships. There were times that I made it almost impossible for us to fight fair. Before he even said anything, my brain would fill in what I just *knew* was coming because of all of the losers I had been with. My past relationships had left me with so much baggage, baggage I didn't realize was taking a toll on us. He was so patient, but even then, I don't think he stood a fair chance.

I'm not giving him a full pass, because he wasn't perfect either. But who is?

If there was a hint of a squabble, I was always terrified he would leave me—so I would tell him to go, before he could. I would do exactly what my therapist always told me not to do: threaten to leave, call him names, and go to bed angry. I needed to have the upper hand to thwart my fear of abandonment. I was terrified of confrontation with a boyfriend after past experiences, so when he was adamant about talking through our fights, I would put in my headphones and ignore him completely. And there's a big difference between taking time to cool down and basically ghosting your relationship.

In hindsight, I had no right to be an interloper in my friends' relationships—or anyone's for that matter. I didn't know any better than they did. My relationship was no more perfect than the ones I was judging.

The Breakup

IN EVERY RELATIONSHIP, the honeymoon phase will at some point come to an end. In the aftermath, the reality of who you really are as a couple can be a harsh slap in the face. You both had an extremely inflated idea of each other, and now it's obvious that neither of you are perfect. The things you overlooked or found endearing about one another have become crystal clear and tiresome.

When my honeymoon phase with Bumble Boy ended, we quickly digressed into the complacency phase. I didn't want to fall even further into the glorified roommates phase like I had done in a previous relationship. Making our relationship work took a backseat to lounging all day in our sweats, keeping the same Postmates order on lock, and never leaving the couch. When you start spending every waking moment with someone not really *doing* anything proactive, you can start to get on each other's nerves. Like, *really* get on each other's nerves.

This didn't happen overnight. We started fighting a lot, sometimes over money and sometimes over nothing at all. There was a period of time we were both just depressed, unhappy people wallowing in our own and each other's paralyzing unhappiness. The thing is, I was empathetic to his feelings and what he was going through in his own life at that time. I knew what it felt like to hit a slump and hope that your partner could understand and work through it with you. I wanted to do for him what he had previously done for me.

We got to a point where I was just exhausted from the relationship and so was he. There was so much love between us that I stayed hopeful. I tried to convince myself that we were going through a phase that would resolve itself. I've always said that I believe love is not effortless; it's effort*ful*. Relationships take work. I was putting in the work, but I wasn't getting 100 percent from him. By the end, I wasn't giving 100 percent either. At that point it became unhealthy for us to remain a couple.

Ultimately, I ripped the Band-Aid off and broke up with him. (As I mentioned before, I've found that guys rarely break up with girls. They leave us to do the dirty work.)

The problem after that was our living situation. After the breakup, we continued to live together for another four months. I was preparing to buy a house and waiting to move into it, and I wasn't going to just kick him out of the apartment we shared together. After all, he was still my best friend.

During that period, some of that time was spent apart; sometimes neither of us wanted to see each other or even speak to each other. But other times we spent time together as a family with our dogs—and yes, we would still sleep together. I was still attracted to him. I still had feelings for him. I still loved him.

Even after we moved out and didn't even live together anymore, the havoc continued. I tried to date here and there, but my heart was with him. My head told me to get out, my heart told me not to give up. It was messy and confusing. After years in a serious relationship, we led such intertwined lives. We had lived together, we had dogs together, we had a *life* together.

Yes, I had imagined my whole life, over and over, about how each new guy was the one I was going to marry—but I *really* thought Bumble Boy was the one. When I met him, it felt like everything I had gone through in life was necessary so that I could meet this person. My person. To be wrong, yet again, was devastating. It was hard to accept that our lives might be going in different directions.

We would have a few great days in a row where I felt everything could be repaired. Maybe I made a mistake breaking up with him? Maybe we should get back together? But the fourth morning would roll around and we would go at it again. It always began with some stupid quick verbal jab, an indignant word inserted for no reason, or an out-of-the-blue blowup. We just couldn't communicate anymore, and being right became more important than fixing the issues.

The hardest part of making a clean break was that without some unforgivable transgression, something I could point to, I always wondered if there was something left to salvage.

There came a point, though, when I realized I'd stopped putting my career and my goals first because I was drowning in his lack of direction and our arguments. I just wanted to stop *fighting*. It took such a toll on me that there were days I didn't want to get out of bed. It was debilitating.

At the same time, we had outside people, friends of mine, making matters worse. They were very vocal in expressing their disappointment in me and him for not moving on. Had they never been through a breakup before? It's not always cut and dry. I could have understood some impatience on their part, but they didn't stop there. They found it OK to insult him and our relationship and call me a liar.

It was so infuriating to me that all it made me want to do was defend and protect him. Their outside meddling only pushed us closer together. They became the common enemy for us to project our anger and hurt feelings onto. At the end of the day, he and I always had each other's backs.

Trying to move on was extremely difficult. I was ready, but I felt so much guilt and I didn't want to hurt him. I tried to put myself in his shoes—how hard it would be for him to think of me with someone else or see me with someone else. But also, the thought of *him* with anyone else made me insanely jealous. Another piece of me wanted him to date someone else, though, so I could feel OK with my decision and start to actually move forward.

In a perfect world, we could both try to move on without throwing it in each other's faces. If I didn't hear from him for a few days my thoughts would run wild: *Is he seeing someone else? Is she better than me? Is* their *relationship easy? Was everything* my *fault?* What if all these issues were mine? It was a really hard thing to unpack.

Ultimately, I did start moving on before he did. I was seeing other people. I was starting to explore a truly separate life from him, but he couldn't detach.

In the end, like I had done so many times to others in the past, he invaded my privacy. This was the first time that this had happened to me. While at my house one day, he took it upon himself to grab my computer and read my iMessages. He found out I was seeing someone else. When he confronted me, I started thinking about all of the other things he might have seen—texts between guys I was talking to, texts between my friends about these guys, texts about him, texts from my friends about their personal lives, texts with embarrassing videos that I should have deleted a long time ago.

What a colossal infringement on my privacy. It made me so angry. I felt violated. Especially since we weren't together anymore. What was he looking for? I now understood just how wrong and invasive it is to intrude upon someone else's personal space. Karma is a bitch.

He messaged me that from that point on we would no longer have any kind of friendship—we could talk only about our dogs. He said he wasn't hurt, he was pissed. He said he was grossed out by me and disgusted with everything about my actions. He said I was not the person he loved, was in love with, or wanted to be with anymore. He said he was done and wanted nothing to do with me.

I know it was just his anger talking. I decided I had to let him express his emotions however he needed to. I also needed to grant us the space we both required.

It was time to finally be *really* single.

She's Making You Crazy

I'LL PREFACE THIS WITH: *yes*, girls talk *incessantly* about our failed or failing relationships with our friends. If we had twenty-five hours in a day, we would talk about it twenty-five hours a day. We would go over the same exact event, topic, problem, or issue regarding the relationship in different ways, with a few added or deleted details each time, until we get the feedback we are looking for from our girlfriends. If it sounds annoying, it is. But . . .

WE ALL DO IT.

When my last relationship was hitting the skids, I finally decided to turn to my best friends for a bitch session with a big bottle of red wine. For a long time there had been a lot of things I'd held back on telling them, because I was still trying to work out and repair my relationship on my own.

I knew that once I'd broken that silence, chances were good that my friends would never look at my man the same way again.

When you tell your friends what's going on, all the difficulties you've been hiding, your hope is that they can be there to support and not judge you. The thing is: all of them know, with almost 100 percent certainty, that you're going to forgive your man—at least once, if not a dozen times.

The difference now? Your friends know. It's out there. You can't put the toothpaste back in the tube. You'll say you were just in a bad mood and tell your friends to forget all those things you told them. But now they're forced to hang out with the guy you love who *they* now despise—because of what *you* told them.

It's a mindfuck, but guys, if you have a wife or girlfriend just know that all of her female friends pretty much know everything and hate you and think you're a dirtbag. I mean, they know *everything*. But your significant other, in confiding in her friends, is hoping that they can see past your flaws and trust her to make her own decisions.

I can't tell you how many times I've sat with my friends after fights with their boyfriends: he left that wet towel on the bathroom floor, or he didn't answer her texts last night, or he didn't pick her up from the airport on time, or boys' night lasted longer than he had promised, or he was a dick to her on her birthday, or he was condescending to her by using big words she didn't know, or she had a drink dumped on her head by her boyfriend on vacation. I even have friends who have been cheated on and made the difficult decision to stay in the relationship. I have always been there for them, listened for hours on end, and tried to only give advice when asked. I knew the unspoken rules of female friendships.

But for some reason, *my* venting had an expiration date. And they ditched me because my love life wasn't picture-perfect.

Why is it that some girlfriends think they know what's best for you? Not just *think* they know, but *know* they know, and *know* they have *all* the right answers?

I like confiding in my friends. I like asking for advice. I *also* like making my own decisions. If it's a mistake, let it be my mistake. Let me learn these lessons on my own. These girls would interject and even argue with me about who I should be seeing, when I should stop seeing someone, or who is best for me.

It isn't always just about my love life either. Sometimes I feel judged about every decision I make. We're all different! I'm going to wear something they might not wear, or listen to music they don't like, or move somewhere they don't think I should. Let me live.

After my last relationship ended, I finally started flirting with a new guy. I was getting my mojo back! One day, my ex came by to see the dogs when a girlfriend was over at my house. He and I were having a great day; we were civil, cordial even, and smiling.

She wasn't a fan of that.

She said she "liked" my ex but thought it was best for me not to see him. Are you fucking kidding me? What did she want me to do, tie the dogs up with a leash to the front porch so he didn't enter my house when he came to get them?

My friend then proceeded to text the guy I was recently talking to, asking him if he knew that I still talk to my ex and that he was over at my house. The new guy *did* know, and he immediately sent me a screenshot of their text exchange to show me what my friend was saying. In the texts, she kept repeating how much it bothered *her* that my ex was around and that if *she* wasn't OK with it, this new guy shouldn't be either. He told her he wasn't bothered by it at all, and that I could handle myself.

I couldn't believe the audacity of my friend. I was livid. What was her end goal? To potentially ruin something brand new I was exploring, yet claim her intentions were pure? The whole situation was none of her business.

Take it down a notch, girl. We are not in a relationship. *You* are not my boyfriend. I was just liberated from one. Now, release me from your insufferable judgment.

The emancipation of Kristen Doute.

PART FOUR

❧

Kickin' It Single

26

Sexting

WE SHOULD DISCUSS THE dick pic. This world has many wonderful things: a beautiful sunset, a walk on the beach, a love letter, a poem, but a surprise dick pic is not one of them. Guys: quit sending us unsolicited dick pics. If you continue to do so, just know that your dick pic might get out there on social media and ultimately become a prop for a sketch comedy show. (If it makes you feel any better, the sketch comedy show will be taken *very seriously*.)

Even worse than the dick pic is the dick *video*. If you haven't received one of those, I envy you. The dick video I once received is burned into my brain for eternity, like *The Blair Witch Project*.

Videos are a hard no—unless he's your husband, I'm guessing. I don't know, I don't have one. (But honestly that might be grotesque as well. I'll ask my married friends.)

When you dip your toe back into the dating pool with twenty-first-century technology, there are a lot of ways to get dragged into a sexting relationship.

Guys, listen. No girl really wants to sext unless you've talked about it beforehand. It's weird. It's creepy. It's unwelcome. If you read the conversation back later, you'll probably notice we were trying to dump cold water on the conversation the whole time.

DICK PIC SENDER

Did you get my text?

I'm home alone

ME

Did you see my Instagram stories?

I came home to watch porn

Where were you guys at?

I can't remember the porn star that looks like you, I'm frustrated

What are you doing for Labor Day Weekend?

Are you looking at what I sent you

I'm thinking about you

Love that

A couple of us are going to Palm Springs, should be fun

Tell me you want to see it and I'll send it again

Palm Springs is nice this time of year

You still didn't say anything about the pictures

[something absolutely filthy]

Really?

Oh my god, go to bed.

How about damn you look hot

Or you can't text because your hands are elsewhere.

Instead it's like oh yeah just an average pic

[more filth]

LOL, I'm laughing so hard right now

If I was there, you wouldn't be laughing

[some REALLY filthy sexting]

If you're staying up to get off, I'm not helpful

I sent it again

Did you get it?

I guess you didn't like them

I saw them.

I get it now

Can we talk about anything else

• • •

Guess not.

Two days later I did get another text from Dick Pic Sender:

> Just delete them if you don't mind

> I can't imagine how pics like that don't turn someone on, but you learn something new every day.

YES. Please. Learn it. Everybody, learn it. It does not turn anyone on. Guys are ruthless and they can be idiots, but honestly, this should be simple: the way to a woman's vagina is through her heart. Just tell me all of the romantic things I want to hear, and I'll gladly grab my ankles.

I've never once initiated a sext, but I've kept it going for one or two replies. If I engage, it's only to please him and keep his mind on me until the next time I see him. Mostly it's super weird, so I think the most I've written back was two times.

And just for the record, while we were sexting you back we were probably in our period-friendly yoga pants, with zit cream on, showing your gross texts to our friends while we sat together and binged *Mindhunter.*

Hit It and Quit It

WHAT'S A BOOK ABOUT dating without a chapter on one-night stands?

We all think we can handle them, and we *all* can't. Well, I guess I don't want to speak for *everybody* here—but I've seen many a friend after a one-night stand checking her phone the whole next day like it was her full-time job, just in case the guy *did* happen to fall in love with her.

Before you imagine I'm out just meeting strangers at bars and taking them home, let me be clear: I will make out with strangers, but I only have sex with friends. (I know what you're thinking, but let's move along; that was at least fifty pages ago.)

My one and only one-night stand was a disaster, as most of them turn out to be. It wasn't a disaster in the way you might think. It was a disaster because my one-night stand wanted to stretch it out into a two-day event. My one-night stand would not vacate the premises.

The night before, my friends and I were on the prowl. Wing-women in full force, we were all down to have a good night out and maybe meet some hot single guys. We were given a tip from the party patrol to hit up the Hyde nightclub. These make-out bandits always knew where the hot single men gathered.

We pregamed at my friend's place, so we were already lit by the time we made it past the bouncer. We had been inside for not even ten minutes when we basically scattered like pigeons to scour the potential prey. We didn't want to stay too long if there were no prospects. While one friend hit the dance floor, another joined a bottle service table and I beelined for the bar. This wasn't really my scene, but I was on a mission.

He was covered in tattoos with a *giant* blue mohawk. Not a metrosexual faux-hawk but a full-on shaved-on-the-sides, ten-inch-tall, spikey, Smurf-blue mohawk. He wasn't physically my type, but my type hadn't been working out for me thus far, so I was down for something new.

He was talkative, charismatic, and gave me free drinks . . . because, well, he was the bartender. And he probably wanted to get laid. By the end of the night? I did too.

He asked if I wanted to hang out after his shift, so I sent my girlfriends on their way and I stuck around until closing. I let him drive me back to my place and invited him in.

We walked in and before I could even kick the door shut he was all over me, ready to go. He threw me on the living room couch, already unsnapping his giant silver belt buckle.

The sex was . . . fine? It certainly wasn't mind blowing. I mean, I couldn't exactly run my fingers through his hair—I had nothing to grab on to. And there was no foreplay: it was a total wham-bam-thank-you-ma'am.

When we woke up the next morning, I prayed I would turn to the left and he would be gone. But he and his blue mohawk were still there. I realized at that moment I couldn't even remember his name.

Is it too slutty to ask for his name now? Did he have a license in his jeans balled up on the floor by my bathroom? What if he caught me going through his wallet?

What happens now? Does he just get up and walk out? Do I make him breakfast? Do I thank him? Does he thank me? Do we exchange bows and phone numbers?

My first one-night stand was raising too many questions for my hungover state.

I quietly got up so as not to wake him. I tiptoed to the bathroom to brush my teeth and remove my makeup plus the one fake lash that was still intact. I took a long, hot shower hoping he had quietly let himself out by the time I was done.

He hadn't.

I crept to the living room and watched TV on mute, with closed captioning.

When he finally did get up, he walked right up to me with just his boxers on. He kissed me on the forehead and said, "Good morning, beautiful." Then he flopped down on the couch next to me and asked if we could put on *CSI*. *He wants to watch CSI first thing in the morning? Is he plotting my murder?* I didn't actually know anything about this man.

He pontificated for hours on subjects that were annoying—things like hunting, trucks, and bartending at Hyde. I tried to be patient, but we had nothing in common, and I couldn't take it anymore. At this point, desperate for a conversation starter, I thought about asking him his last name—but then I remembered I couldn't remember his first name, and also, I didn't care.

How can I get him to leave? He was already trying to make plans with me for that night.

Then he dropped the bomb. This dude voted for Trump. *Trump!* Why the hell didn't he say that hours ago? *Last night* even? That very pertinent information could have saved me from making a regrettable choice last night and sitting through hours of dreadful, awkward conversation all day *today.*

I grabbed his boots from my room, handed them over to him where he sprawled across my couch, and said, "Last night was fun. I don't know the rules of a one-night stand, but I'm pretty sure it means *one night*, so you can leave now." There was no exchange of bows, or numbers, but he *did* thank me as he walked out.

Maybe rushing into relationships hasn't been so bad after all, if one-night stands are like *that.* Definitely not my style, and I won't be doing it again.

Friends with Benefits

YOU KNOW THE OLD notion that men and women can't be friends? I think we can, but only after we get the sex out of the way. Like I said, I don't have sex with strangers. I mean, I did one time. But just once. (No judgment if you do it often! I just know it's not for me.)

I'm a Renaissance woman with my own roster of go-tos. Girls can have little black books too, you know! "Friends with benefits" is not only a possible dynamic, it's an *imperative* one. We all need an ego boost every once in a while. When you're in the driver's seat as a woman setting the terms of the encounter, it's honestly quite exhilarating. *I* choose. *I* decide. The truth is, not to tell on myself, but I miiiiight just have a few of these at the moment.

The most important thing in navigating these FWB relationships is to always be up front with them. Do not treat these guys the way guys so often treat girls. Stress that no, this is *not* a date. This is a hangout. No, this is *not* us forming an exclusive long-lasting relationship. This is us here and now, having fun, having sex.

Surfer Dude was a fun FWB. He never wanted anything serious and said he'd roll with the rule "If you don't want *anyone* to know, don't tell *anyone*." And I didn't tell anyone, until now.

I called another FWB on the phone just now to ask him what nickname he wanted. He replied, "Mr. Perfect." We'll just go with that. Mr. Perfect says he doesn't believe he's hot; he thinks he's funny. I think he's hot *and* funny. Still waters run deep. We kissed one drunken night and suddenly we were FWBs. He's definitely a prospect, on some level, but we've also been in the same friend group for years. At this point that's a boat I'm just not willing to rock, but hey—I'll float on it for a minute now and again.

I was introduced to Bachelor through a friend at a West Hollywood restaurant. He lived out of town but frequented L.A. for work. Bachelor was younger than me and absolutely adorable. I knew we could be friends, but he was definitely not boyfriend material. He knew it too. We got drunk, he came back to my house, we made out, he slept over. That was it. He left for the airport the next morning—and left his watch on my bedroom floor—but we stay in touch through text. I returned the watch ASAP through our mutual friend, because I didn't need anything lingering. He's a great kisser and hopefully we will be great FWBs.

Then there's a guy in New York and a guy in Michigan. You need to keep your options open, especially when you travel a lot. If you're in any one place a lot of the time, make sure you've got a friend there.

This doesn't make me some kind of undercover hoe who should be ashamed of myself. If guys can do it, we can do it too. This is called being S-I-N-G-L-E. It's the twenty-first century, ladies.

I Kissed a Girl

MAKING OUT WITH YOUR hot girlfriends is the ultimate drunk-girl-at-the-bar party trick. Chances are when this happens, the girls are both straight and it is 100 percent attention-seeking behavior. And, it's going to keep happening, because it works! It's a powerful tool in eliciting the male attention girls are seeking in the first place. It's also a huge ego boost. Even straight women can find other women attractive—we can all agree we are just the prettier sex. Women have an extremely strong bond and aren't afraid to show our admiration and affection for one another. And sometimes it's just fun. We all like flirting, but there's less pressure when you know kissing can just be kissing.

I've kissed many friends like that, where it's just playful. But I've also taken a real dip in the lady pond once or twice, though I never fully swam around. I don't want to close any doors, because I've only had heterosexual relationships thus far in my life but right now I guess I would consider myself . . . heteroflexible? Mostly straight, but open to sexual experimentation. I like men, but I'm not ruling out other options.

My second experience with another woman was with a sexually fluid girlfriend of mine in Los Angeles. She suggested we have a threesome together with my boyfriend. She said she wanted to help me out, because at that particular time in my relationship, my boyfriend seemed to have no interest in me, in having sex with me, or generally anything that involved touching me. I figured *why not* at that point—I'd try anything.

She wasn't just *anything*, though. To be fair, I thought she was hot. And I knew she was into me and not him. And she had already told me in the past that she wanted to hook up with me.

I decided I was into having this experience whether he joined or not.

My friend devised a plan to come over before a night out to get ready together. We both showered and put on our sexy, short silk robes and lathered up with lotion in the bedroom right in front of him, while he lounged watching *Through the Wormhole with Morgan Freeman* on our bed. We giggled, flirted with each other, and picked out the sluttiest dresses in my closet to hold up to see what he thought. At first, he seemed a little perplexed about what was happening, but after we modeled a few hot outfits for him, he seemed to get into it. Guys can be so simple. She playfully flipped up the back of my robe, smacked my butt, and told me how hot I looked, loud enough for him to pay attention.

We continued this impassioned flirting the whole night at the bar. I was surprised by how much I was into it. I wasn't worried anymore about him, where he was, or what he was doing.

Then, out of nowhere, he suddenly grabbed me and kissed me at the bar—in public. Of *course,* the first time in *months* he'd shown me any public display of affection was when I didn't care anymore.

I wanted to be with *her* that night.

We got back to the apartment and got right to it. She pulled me into my bedroom, we kissed, and we immediately got each other naked. She patted the mattress to my right, inviting my boyfriend to lie next to me like, *Hi, here's your girlfriend and she's naked. Do something about it.* He stripped down to his boxer briefs and sprung onto the bed. As she and I got into it, he kissed me and reached his hand over toward her. She grabbed his arm and gently pushed it away, told him that this was a spectator sport. Either he could watch us or she would watch him with me.

He didn't get it. She wanted *me*, not a threesome with my boyfriend. But he was so selfish that he didn't feel one night could be about me. Yes, initially we had been planning a threesome, but she and I were no longer interested in having him between us. The situation got awkward, and it didn't go that far, because I was totally in my head about everything. We did cuddle, though, and that was nice.

Another time, I took a dip in the lady pond quite literally . . . in a hot tub.

This one sort of falls on one of my FWBs. He took me to a party with some of our friends and introduced me to a hot girl he'd been platonic friends with for years. From the beginning of the night, he kept remarking how delighted he was that we got along so well, and that he just knew we would be fast friends. He *knew* we would like each other. He was right; we did get along, and we had the best time dancing, laughing, and taking an abundance of blurry photos.

He playfully teased her about how she had to go out earlier to buy a dress before the party that night because she didn't own one. And we all laughed as she tripped and fell because she couldn't walk in her heels. She was a tomboy, even though she looked girly that night, and he kept implying that she and he both played for the same team. He said maybe she would find a girl that night to take home. The comments felt pointed in my direction.

When we finally left the party, the three of us went back to my house for a tipsy dip in my hot tub. I let her borrow a bathing suit and poured us all a drink. Once we were in the jacuzzi it took less than minutes for her and me to start making out. About twenty minutes later, I realized we'd been so hot and heavy that my FWB had disappeared, and I had no idea when it happened. *Where did he go?*

I got out of the hot tub, found my phone, and called him. He had watched us for a little while and then left and went home. He was upset. I didn't get it. We had even invited him to join us at one point!

I apologized for "ignoring" him, talked him out of his pouty mood, and asked him to come back over. It wasn't like we had meant to hurt his feelings or leave him out—but hadn't he been hinting toward me hooking up with her for the whole night?

It turned out that she, too, identified as straight. I don't even know if she'd been with other women in the past. He hadn't been dropping hints to me at all. The inside joke between them was that her tomboy style was an indication of her secret lesbian preference, and his teasing wasn't about him wanting to see her with me at all. He turned into a sensitive sunflower because *she* wound up getting the attention that he wanted from me. That's on him.

The lady pond is still pretty mysterious to me, but the water's fine . . . and I wouldn't mind taking another dip.

The Casual Dating Minefield

SOMETIMES CASUAL DATING can become complicated when one of you decides you're interested in something less casual and more serious. If you aren't careful, and you're spending all your time together and having *so* much *fun*, a casual FWB sort of thing can transform into a serious relationship within a few weeks without anyone really deciding. This dating trajectory is a real hassle when you're trying to stay single.

I'm a serial monogamist and I also tend to spend a lot of my time with someone when I like-like them. When I say a lot, I mean *a lot*; I might text you twenty times a day, FaceTime you three times a week, and dial you up without hesitation if I have a passing thought or a quick question.

This particular guy I was talking to came over in the afternoon one day after sleeping over the night before. I thought we were going to have lunch and a casual afternoon hookup sesh while watching *The Jinx* on HBO. But, he wanted to "talk."

He said if there was honestly a 0 percent chance that I saw potential for a more serious relationship, he wanted out now. He couldn't do it anymore, just a friends-with-benefits relationship with me. I had thought he would *dig* this arrangement—what guy wouldn't? We'd been buddies for over four years, we were becoming closer friends, and now we had sex . . . often. Without any further relationship obligations on his part.

I didn't know what he was up to or who he was dating when I wasn't around. And the thing is, I didn't care.

It was simple, until it became not-so-simple. It was obvious he liked me.

Though I was having the best time with him, my head was telling me to be smart. I knew I wasn't ready for another relationship so soon, and I kept telling myself that. At the same time, I didn't want to end what we had going on, at least not so abruptly. So . . . I told him there was a 1 percent chance. That was the carrot he needed to hold on to.

That 1 percent quickly rose to 3 percent over the course of the week. It became our inside joke. (*Oh no, this could be a sign. We already have inside jokes.*) We weren't *really* moving up a percentage point every single day, but we were spending a lot more time together, having a blast, and I thought he deserved the ego boost—3 percent felt about right overall.

He was smart, funny, driven, and kind; plus, our sexual chemistry was on point. He made me feel special and was constantly trying to impress me. But, I wasn't ready to commit, and I definitely didn't want to end up hurting him by rushing into a relationship I couldn't handle. It was easier to keep my guard up and keep him at bay, on the FWB level. But once you're sleeping with one person on the reg, it can start to feel less like hanging and banging and more like . . . actual dating.

He was also different from any of the guys I'd dated in the past. My friends said he was good for me. *He has his shit together, he's driven, he has a five-year plan (even a ten-year plan), and he owns a home!* He was rational, communicative, and didn't play games.

But there were a few complications surrounding this particular guy. We shared a friend group, and I didn't want to mess with that dynamic. *What if it doesn't work out?* Could we safely go back to being just friends, or would it destroy the group? What if I met someone else and wanted to give them a shot? *What if I mess this up?* The more I allowed the questions to build, the more I wanted to just run from this situation.

But the truth is, I really liked him. Maybe that was the biggest problem of all. Why did he have to *talk* about it? Once he said it, it was out there. Then it couldn't be ignored. The feelings between us were definitely there. *Fuck.* I was afraid, because I could see how I could easily fall into old patterns. I don't want a boyfriend right now. Hopefully a 3 percent chance is enough for this great guy, for now.

There are still so many people I want to make out with in life.

The Holy Grail

THERE IS ALWAYS ONE GUY from your past who lingers in the memory, a guy you would drop everything to be with. Just for the *chance* to be with him, even. Most likely you never really dated, and if you did date it was casual and it just faded out, because one of you moved, or it was long distance, or whatever. No big breakup, no big fight. He is your Holy Grail, the treasure on the horizon you can never quite reach.

You think about this guy more than you'll admit, and the thought of you two finally ending up together, like something out of a rom-com or a fairy tale, keeps you sane through the hard times in your current relationship. You keep in touch with him, carefully, and your significant other thinks he's just an old friend. You *never* tell your current boyfriend or lover you used to date the Holy Grail, or that you have any interest in him at all. This is your secret.

A simple text from the Holy Grail makes you smile. A funny meme from him makes you giggle. He's never outwardly flirty in text messages when you're in a relationship with someone else, but he knows how to say things that you are able to read between the lines.

If you're of a certain age (let's say over thirty) and you find yourself single again, it will of course strike you that it might be time to give this whole thing a real go with the Holy Grail. After all, you assume he's clearly felt the same way about *you* your whole life. You think you are also the one that got away. You're sure he wonders about you constantly.

You think he feels the same way about you. He doesn't.

My Holy Grail was everything I had ever dreamed of. His sense of humor was beyond; he was lighthearted and hysterically funny. He was kind, charming, tall, and drop-dead gorgeous. His smile could light up any room, and he had this mantra about leading everything in life with love. He knew how to make me feel so special. When we were together, I was the only girl in the world. The butterflies I felt for him were impossible to disregard any time he gave me the attention I had been longing for.

But when we weren't together, for him it was like I didn't exist. Not only was he hard to get, but he was impossible to keep. He popped in and out of my life at his convenience, and I allowed him to. *Why is he sending me mixed signals when I'm being so crystal clear?* I would try to stay strong and stop contacting him, but he still made me weak in the knees.

Our "relationship" was very black and white. There was no gray area except for the random texts, which were few and far between.

Here's an example of what my Holy Grail would do to keep me on the hook: We kept texting trying to make plans while we were both traveling a lot. We always seemed to miss each other. I told him I was going to Vegas, then to Denver, but I would be back the following week and we should try to get together. The *very* Sunday I landed in Denver, he texted me asking me if I wanted to come over and watch a movie, to Hulu and chill. (He still uses my passwords. I . . . should change those.) I was crushed! Of all of the days and times. I contemplated flying straight home to hang out with him, but then I decided this gave me the upper hand. I *wasn't* available, for once! Hah! I would be the distancer rather than the pursuer, play hard to get, make him long for me. I told him I was out of town but was *really* looking forward to seeing him when I got back.

Days later, it suddenly dawned on me. We'd had a whole conversation about our travel schedule before I went to Denver, with dates included. He knew I was out of town when he asked me to come over. He *knew* I wasn't available and that's exactly why he reached out. Very. Fucking. Calculated.

The Perfect Boyfriend

He didn't want to show his hand. He wanted me to stay on the hamster wheel.

Another thing about Holy Grails is that they never, ever call. They only text, or sometimes slide into your DMs. Voice would be too intimate. He also only cares about you if he thinks you've moved on to someone else. Then he makes his presence known, to keep you hanging on.

Sometimes I would get fed up. So did I "end things" with him often? Yeah, I did. Too many times, after days of not hearing back from him, I would send paragraph upon paragraph, with full conviction, stating that I deserved more and we needed to go back to being *just friends without benefits.* I was like a teenager again, demanding attention. I felt stupid every time I hit send on one of those texts, knowing it should have died in my Notes app.

But I didn't *want* to play hard to get. I wanted a relationship with him. I couldn't play hard to get even when I tried. All of the work I did on myself, telling myself I was worth more, would dissipate with a simple 2:00 AM text from him.

Was I his booty call? Oh God, I was totally his booty call. Day or night, whenever he was in town—and his job entailed touring often. I couldn't stand being just his pen pal when he was gone. I found myself screenshotting our texts and sending them to a girlfriend, begging for advice. Do I play hard to get? Do I act coy? How do I get him to love me? Of all the men who'd made me crazy, he was maybe making me the craziest.

And he knew exactly how to reel me back in. Every. Single. Time.

Hold on, I'm gonna shoot him a text right now to tell him I'm writing about him. Let's see what he says back.

Ah, this time it was pretty immediate. He said, "Oh boy, that makes me nervous."

IT SHOULD.

I was a human yo-yo, with the string tied loosely around his finger so I could keep spinning when he let me go. *I'm right here! Pull me back up! I've been waiting for you all of my life!!*

Insert facepalm here.

I made plans for us. This could so easily work. There was always room in my heart for him.

Self-love at 1 million percent is required to deal with having a Holy Grail; otherwise, he will absolutely drive you insane.

Finally, after ages of touch-and-go back-and-forth, I came to the realization that the whole thing was a facade. He never wanted us to be an actual couple. What he wanted was for me to pine over him, to put him on a pedestal. He wanted me to think he was this great guy—the *greatest* guy. He wanted me to quest for the Holy Grail for the rest of my damn life. He probably had a lot of other girls just like me, a dozen Chicks of the Round Table riding out on horseback with our minds set on finding him and bringing him back to Camelot.

He was a true master of manipulation. In some ways he was actually the worst of them all. His indifference was worse for my self-esteem than the exes who hated me or whom I had grown to hate, because I was so invested and *he* had absolutely no emotional stake in our faux relationship. Unlike every other guy I had dated, the Holy Grail never had any real feelings. Not for me, and maybe not for anyone.

Anyway, when you realize the Holy Grail was never a knight in shining armor, you can see all at once that he's a wolf in sheep's clothing. The biggest liar of them all. The one man you absolutely *must* let go of to move on and live your life.

PART FIVE

Kumbaya, Bitches

32

My Ex, His Girl, My Friends

RELATIONSHIPS ARE HARD. Breakups are hard. Being friends with your exes is even harder.

In my experience, how hard or easy that will be depends on the nature of the breakup and the amount of time that has passed. I've had two really tricky ex-boyfriend relationships that have turned, with time and patience, into genuine friendships.

One of them you might be super familiar with, since we shared our breakup with the world. I dated that particular ex for one-fifth of my adulthood. Breaking up after dating for six out of my thirty years on earth was a lot to digest. But eventually, we *did* become friends again.

When we broke up, he started dating someone else immediately—or, you know, maybe they were already secretly dating;

they don't ever have to cop to it, but I can theorize about it in my own book!!—and now I love them both. Crazy, right? To be honest, right now he and his girlfriend, that same girl, are two of the most supportive and loving friends I have in my life.

So *how* did we come to be friends again? It wasn't easy. It was the road less traveled, that's for damn sure. The two of them had to really recognize and trust that not only was I over him, but I was also over making their lives a living hell. That took work on my part. Sometimes I had to tape my mouth shut for about ten minutes as a lesson in self-control. (Scotch tape works for this, and it's very affordable.) They probably wished I'd done it for a few days at a time.

I had to take my ego out of it. I had to humble myself. The social purgatory I was living in with them wasn't doing anyone any favors. I made a choice to let everything go, because whether or not I thought those rumors about an illicit rendezvous or two behind my back had been true or not, it didn't matter anymore. A girl can't actually *steal* someone's boyfriend. He made a free-willed choice to leave me, and a free-willed choice to be with her. I needed to let them be happy.

It took a lot of time, and it took a lot of personal growth. And just because *I* got to a place where I wasn't angry anymore, where I wasn't jealous anymore . . . that didn't mean *they* were over all the things I'd done to try to sabotage them. It didn't mean they were ready to trust me, or befriend me. They weren't ready for me to just show up at their apartment with a casserole or something, though I did know where they lived. After all, I used to live there.

They needed to find their own path to forgiving me.

We slowly began hanging out in group settings, and eventually we could do it without any ill will. We could go on vacation (or just film for work) all together without feeling the need to side-eye. Over time, we didn't have to fake being nice, and the three of us were fine in smaller social settings without the group as a buffer.

The thing is, once I really let my walls come down and got to know this girl, I started to really *like* her. I used to *loathe* her! Loathe the *idea* of her, really, since I hadn't known her very well before it all went down. But we had so much more in common than I ever thought possible. She was actually able to move on before my ex did, once I apologized to her sincerely. It takes a strong woman to take responsibility for her actions, but it takes a stronger woman to forgive. I'm grateful she did.

As for my ex, he was still cautious. To be fair to him, it was pretty hard to just let go of my prior crazy antics. He still wasn't ready to let me back in. He liked to keep me roughly one hundred feet away from him and have two or three people between us at all times. It wasn't like a restraining order or anything hostile. It was more like an unspoken physical and emotional barrier.

Then my ex's dad came into town, and he and all of our friends attended a birthday party together. I kept my distance, respectfully, because I hadn't spoken to his family in years by this point. I was ordering a drink at the bar when my ex and his dad approached me. *What was happening?*

My ex asked me if I had said hello to his dad yet. I hadn't, because, well, because of the informal hundred-foot rule. Was this an olive branch? It was. They both gave me a hug, his dad wished me well, and we did a Jägerbomb together. It was like old times again. I finally felt like the long nightmare was over. I knew then that my ex was ready to move on and forgive me too.

And then I started to really like *him,* as a person, again. My anger had completely dissipated. When I looked at him I was able to appreciate the things I'd loved about him in the beginning, just without romantic feelings attached. I saw him in a different light now. I'm not sure I've ever felt true growth as satisfying as that change.

With the weight lifted, I realized he and his girlfriend were really made for each other. They're so much better for each other than he and I ever could have been. Things that bothered me about him? She finds them endearing. It doesn't faze her when he cries, and he cries *a lot.* She cheers him on when he dresses in drag for special occasions, because—I have to hand it to him—he really commits. She even accepted that he bought a ridiculously expensive motorcycle with a sidecar when they were actively saving for their future. These are things that would make me crazy. Probably a lot of other women, too.

But she speaks his love languages, and I speak his friend language. Now? I can just laugh at these things from afar. I can be happy for them, and I am *so* happy for them.

We now have a strong friendship: supporting each other, defending each other, and always having each other's backs. At this point I can hardly even imagine the fact that he and I used to date, much less that we dated for so long. It's proof that time can heal all wounds, if you work at it.

Co-Parenting

MAKING A CLEAN BREAK from an ex is much harder when you still have something keeping the two of you connected. For me and Bumble Boy, it's our two dogs, Gibson and Bowie. Co-parenting animals is complicated—so complicated, in fact, that there are whole self-help books written about it. And I'll definitely need someone to buy me one of those books for Christmas this year, because this chapter in my life has been extremely exhausting to navigate.

It's not that I don't want to share our "kids" with him; I do. I know he loves them just as much as I do, and he's a great dog dad. It's about the boundaries. I'm a lousy boundary-setter, and when I do try to set them, I'm an even worse boundary-follower.

The thing is, I sometimes feel like he uses our dogs as leverage. Leverage to see me, and leverage to continue to be an active participant in my life. Maybe, too, there have been times when *I've* subconsciously used them as leverage to make him come around.

Sometimes I just need help, and I'm not very good at asking for it, let alone accepting it.

We're fortunate that we have a dog trainer who not only takes the boys on romps and works with them on discipline but also can board them overnight. But if my schedule is busy and I need help, I try to give Bumble Boy the first opportunity to take them if he's free. That involves scheduling drop-off and pickup. Sometimes we like hanging out as a family again, taking them on walks and out to lunch. It's fun for them, and fun for us, but it's also fraying at those boundaries I've tried to set. It's my fault, really; I'm an optimist.

He somehow instinctively knows when I have someone else over, and that's always the time he is most interested in coming over to see the dogs or pick them up. When he has our kids for a while, it sometimes feels like he's holding them hostage until he can see me again.

On Bowie's birthday, I invited my ex to celebrate at my place. He came over and he stayed for three days. I know that this is partly my fault; I'm sure I gave him mixed signals, and we fell right back into our old routine—laughing, talking, cooking together, playing Scrabble, cuddling with the dogs, and watching football all day on a rainy Sunday. Rainy days were our jam!

All of the great moments like those reminded me of how great we were as a family. And for years, first and foremost, he had been my best friend. So even if we both had accepted that the relationship didn't work, it was difficult to drop the romantic feelings we had for one another, especially when we were still so connected.

But then it had been three days, and I realized we'd fallen back into some sort of relationship again! And then I snapped. I can't go back there. I do want us to remain close, if it's possible, but we are not a couple anymore, and I need my space.

BOUNDARIES, DOUTE!

The arrangement is tricky, yes, but there are also upsides to co-parenting. Their little ears perk and their eyes light up when they hear the word "Daddy." I *want* them to spend time with him. I have friends with doggies from broken homes, and I would be devastated if I didn't see Gibson and Bowie anymore, so I would never do that to him or to them. I would never take them away from him, and I'll always make it work.

That said, making it work has proven complicated for whatever kind of relationship this has become, or whatever one we're now trying to have. One day when I was really sad, I didn't want to see him but I asked him to pick them up. They didn't deserve to see me sad. Call me crazy, but I firmly believe our puppy children take on the energy that surrounds them. They know when you're sad and feel it when you fight. (Plus, I wasn't in the mood to take them on a W-A-L-K, but I knew he would.) Now, these dogs are my emotional support animals; they would happily cling to me and kiss me until I felt better, but that's not their job. I want healthy, active fur babies who aren't soaking in any bad vibes.

Last year, I was about to hop on a plane home from my birthday party in Nashville when Gibson, our Yorkie, got seriously mauled by a huge pit bull at the dog park. Bumble Boy bolted to the veterinary hospital and had to handle it all on his own while I was in full panic mode half a country away. I can't imagine having to manage that alone; he was my hero. Gibson survived, but we were devastated so it immediately brought us back together. This wasn't a DVR box I needed to get back from an ex's apartment, this was our baby. I don't know what I would've done without him. It's not just about co-parenting in a situation like that; it's about history.

We are trying to remain friends—even, dare I say, best friends—because there is a reason he was in my life to begin with. I don't want to ever forget those reasons. So it's not always easy, because when we're solid, we're solid, but that just isn't constant enough for us to be together.

We might not have it all figured out just yet, but in the meantime, at least we have two very happy dogs.

The Boomerang

SOMETIMES THE WHOLE WORLD shifts under your feet. Sometimes you feel totally alone. Maybe your best friends have abandoned you, maybe you feel like nobody understands you, and maybe—definitely—you don't feel like yourself. In fact, all you want to do is find yourself again.

When Bumble Boy and I broke up and I moved into my new house, I had a lot of alone time to think. As I started accepting this was going to be an entirely new, unknown, and unnerving chapter for me, I got an unexpected text message from a man I thought had left my life forever. We'd lost touch after he got married, and I hadn't spoken to him in a decade.

A nostalgic trip down memory lane, reminiscing about simpler times, was exactly what the doctor ordered.

In a strange twist of fate, we both seemed to be in the same confusing place in our lives at the same time.

When we'd first met, I was a freshman in high school. It was two months into the school year, and in first period there was always one empty seat to my right. One day, this gorgeous, magnificent specimen glided across the classroom and sat down in that empty seat next to me. He didn't have a book, a pencil, a backpack, anything. It was so hot. The only thing he carried was the wafting bouquet of Cool Water cologne, which filled the space he suddenly occupied.

He leaned over to say hello, and I leaned closer to immerse myself in his essence. We smiled and flirted with each other for the entire hour of class. *Instant* chemistry.

Was he new in town? Where had he been for two months? Was he dating anyone? *Had anyone else met him yet?*

I needed to hurry up and claim him before anyone else did. My friends were ruthless, and I had to get to him first.

When the bell rang, I made my move. On the walk from our desks to the classroom door, I got his entire life story. He was a senior and he was supposed to be in this class since the year started. He had a thing called co-op, so he had been working and getting a note to miss the class—but he hadn't really been working, and he got caught, so he had to start coming to school or they would fail him. His loss and my gain! Clearly, this would be the start of a long, fruitful relationship.

Except . . . he only made it to class for one week, and that was it. It wasn't until a year later that we saw each other again.

My friends and I were out looking for something to do. The girls mentioned this guy with his own house was having a house party. Free beer and whatever was in the liquor cabinet; we were 100 percent in. And when we got to the house . . . there he was.

A boomerang I thought had flown away, swinging back into my life.

He was so cool, so chill, like a combination of all the music I listened to. He had the hippie mystique of Roger Waters and the hip-hop swagger of Eminem. He was quiet but somehow still the life of the party. He felt unattainable. I thought I never stood a chance, *especially* when he started dating one of my friends on and off. Even so, I still crushed on him for *years*. (And honestly, so did everyone else.)

Over the years that followed we became party friends, the kind of acquaintances who share a quick hug and pleasantries in passing. I was always invited to his weekend shindigs, and I never turned down the chance to be in the same room with him.

And then one night at our local watering hole, Howell's, I was with a couple of girlfriends when my Boomerang showed up. I still remember it like it was yesterday. He was rocking a gray and black button-down shirt, a black rope necklace (think Ryan from *The O.C.*), and a raw sexual energy I simply couldn't ignore.

The four of us were kicking it, all drinking and having fun, when my two friends had to use the restroom. Typically, I would have joined them for a quick gossip session, but I couldn't pass up this opportunity! Not when my Boomerang was sitting beside me. The second they turned the corner, it was my chance—and I took it.

I grabbed him by the arm and said, "Let's go." He didn't hesitate. We got in his blue VW bug and drove.

We spent the next year becoming so close. We had a friendship that not many knew about, let alone understood. Our chemistry was so intense, and we couldn't keep our hands off of each other—in private. I don't know why we snuck around, but we did. It was something just for us. No one else knew the soft, sweet, sensitive side of him. They didn't know what a brilliant writer and poet he was (and still is). I don't think he felt comfortable being his true self around anyone but me.

And then, as life sometimes has it, we drifted apart. It became a memory, just a moment in time that had been special to me. I moved on and moved away, and he got married and had a family.

I still texted him every year on his birthday, even though I never really received much of a response. Ultimately, I decided to let any deeper feelings go and accept the fact that our lives were just different now.

But here he was again, boomeranging back to me over a decade later. Fate had intervened, and we were both feeling the same way at the same time: out of sorts, alone unexpectedly, and disconnected from our place in the world.

We immediately made plans to travel together.

Being with him made me feel like I was me again. It felt good that after everything I'd been through, this person who'd known me as a teenager still thought I was the same Kristen. The Kristen I had lost. The Kristen who never doubted herself, or her worth.

His faith in me helped me understand that this narrative I'd crafted, the narrative placed on me by all the dudes who had systematically broken down my self-esteem over the years, was false. I *do* deserve love. I *do* deserve attention and affection.

He wanted to be with me again because he really knew the Kristen from Dearborn, a Michigan girl who was nobody. It wasn't about my successes in the time since; it was just about me.

He didn't care about the person everyone thinks I am because they see facets of my life on a reality show. He had always loved me, and still loved me, just the way I really am.

It was just the kind of intervention I needed. I was still so devastated that things hadn't worked out with Bumble Boy, and I was able to extract all those feelings and transfer them onto someone else, someone safe, someone that I knew from back home. My Boomerang. Someone I *knew* I could be vulnerable with, who would handle my emotional state with extreme care.

Of course, I didn't realize just how much I was projecting onto him. In the end our reunion was just a fun escape, nostalgic and comforting, not something that would or could last forever. That wasn't reality. In reality we've grown a lot, and changed a lot, and we are in different places. Deep down we both knew it was never going to work out in the long run, but for a moment we could both be the shelter the other needed in an emotional storm.

I'll always be grateful for what he did for me. He came back into my life and helped me through a difficult transition, and I'm so happy we reconnected. He will always hold a special place in my heart. I needed to rediscover that faith in myself.

But it was time to leave fantasies behind. It was time to start really *dealing* with my own feelings. Time to live in the uncomfortable place of not knowing what's next. To stop running away from my problems and plant myself squarely in the world I'd made for myself, in all its chaos.

On my own.

Taking Care of Me

IT'S NOW BEEN OVER A decade since my first search for enlightenment at that cult indoctrination weekend near LAX, and I'm still on the hunt. Nirvana isn't attained in a day, you know! I have to keep working at it. I've had a few bumps in the road and a lot of major setbacks, but I haven't given up on myself. If you're running in circles, you need to stop and change your path. Life's too short to live the same day twice. If what you're doing isn't working, try something else.

Personally, I am willing to try anything. I mean *anything.*

- I have a personal energy healer and a tarot card reader.
- I host women's moon circles. (I bought a fire pit; we burn our negative feelings under the full moon.)
- Sage, palo santo, cleansing ritual candles, spell kits. You name it, I'll try it.

I recently became interested in Taoism. I'm fascinated by it, in fact. That manipulative Holy Grail guy got me into it at first, but the interest has remained even now that he's a thing of the past. I'm hoping I can learn something valuable from the centuries of philosophy behind it.

There was a period of time where I went to bed every single night listening to Dr. Wayne Dyer's *5 Minutes Before You Fall Asleep* meditation. It's like Xanax, wrapped in a bow, for my soul, but with no side effects! I've made it through an hour-long relaxation playlist, but never *once* have I made it through those five minutes without falling asleep. Hey, if it works it works. (Yes, you should YouTube that *for sure*. RIP, Dr. Dyer.)

Here are a few of my favorite things:

Crystals

When I shop for my crystals, unless I'm going in with a *purpose* I just see what I'm naturally drawn to and then read up on their supposed properties. Sometimes I keep them in my purse. I always have a few on my window sill and by my bed. When I'm feeling extra attuned to the universe, I cleanse them with water in the moonlight before setting my intentions for them.

I did sketch comedy for a brief while, as you may know, and I would always put crystals in my bra before I went on stage, because it made me feel braver and stronger. If I'm wearing a bra, I have crystals in it. I swear it works.

Therapy

I've been in therapy for almost five years. I might be the biggest therapy advocate you've ever met.

Sometimes I go once a week, sometimes twice per month, and there were times when I would just take a break completely, but I've always gone back. I think therapy is the healthiest thing a person can do for themselves. That said, therapy is different for everyone. I had to find a therapist that I connected with.

The first few people I met with, I couldn't eye-roll harder. I would think, *Please, say "How does it make you feel?" one more time. I feel like I need a cocktail and a real therapist.*

I'm just saying it took me a minute to find my match, so if you're in that space, don't be deterred! You have to find the person that you really vibe with. There were days when I was in a great mood and didn't feel I needed to go, but I still did (after a quick stop for sex with an FWB—after all, my therapist told me I have to remember to do things for myself).

Sometimes therapy's just a full-on venting sesh. Other times, we dig deep into my past to sort out the underlying, nitty-gritty stuff that affects me today. (You have now read about basically all of it in this book.) Sometimes I'm just fresh out of fucks and fresh out of feelings, but if you give me a few days I'll have more. See you next week—same crazy time, same crazy channel.

If you're truly willing to give therapy a shot, my advice is to be 100 percent transparent. Don't attempt to fool a therapist to get the answers you want. You can do that with your friends. Plus, why blow through your hard-earned money to lie to a professional? Just to prove your own dumb ego is right.

Witchcraft

By witchcraft, I mean the millennial Hollywood version—the Witches of WeHo version.

I have always believed in the primal elements of the earth. I love being barefoot, and I smoke weed; isn't that enough?

I believe that intention can will things to happen. (Don't try me; I'm in a good space right now.) I only dabble in these practices to prevent harm or wrongdoing, never to bring pain to someone. I will try anything to heal and protect myself, and my friends, from malevolent forces.

One time one of our best friends was cheated on, so we all threw her a "Fuck Him" party to convince her that she dodged a bullet. Then, to really bring the hammer down on her boyfriend, we put a hex on him. To be clear, our intention was not to hurt him in any physical way. Our spell was all about scorning a cheating lover. And I guess it worked: he changed his ways! They got engaged and are now happily married.

Actually, maybe I should look into this witch thing a little more seriously.

Curbing Social Media

Social media can be intoxicating and it can also be the devil. It's draining! Whenever I get too caught up in the comments, or start obsessing over someone's feed, I temporarily delete my apps from my phone. This is a common practice.

Curbing our social media addiction is something I think we all need for our mental well-being.

To block, to mute, or to unfollow? That is the question.

Now, mind you, sometimes I'm not strong enough to just *not look*. The social media society we live in today brings us together as easily as it tears us apart. It messes with your self-image. Do you know how many face-tuning apps there are? Like a million. I have five on my phone in hot rotation.

It's almost impossible to avoid overthinking—who is watching, how many likes and views? And then there are the comments. The never-ending comments from trolls lurking in their caves behind their laptop screens, comments you *know* you shouldn't pay attention to, but you do.

And a lot of it is artifice. Your social media "friend" might post that she's on a yacht in St. Tropez, but she's really sitting on her couch in her tear-stained hoodie, eyes glued to the Domino's Tracker. I had to get over the FOMO, the sugar baby Instagram models with their perfect fake tits, and the rabbit hole of stalking an ex-boyfriend's feed, then stalking every girl he has ever interacted with. (This leads to the worst moment of all: accidentally liking some-thing *real deep* on one of those girls' pages, knowing she probably has her notifications on and that even if you unlike it *immediately* you've still been caught.)

This is not real life, people. *Everyone* exaggerates on social media. We're all putting our best foot forward. What's real is what is happening around you. Put your phone down for five seconds and be present—especially at a concert.

Of course, this is still a work in progress for me, so don't feel bad if it's hard for you. I can post photos of myself makeup-free now, but I still can't fully say good-bye to #filters.

Energy Healing

I originally decided to go to an energy healer after I bought my house. My house was built in 1939, which means a *lot* of folks have laid their heads to rest here—a lot of people I don't need to extract any spiritual energy from. I wanted my new home to be free from anything that might be harmful. The healer I found was extremely beneficial. She closed portals, put a shield around my new abode, and helped an unwelcome ghost guest on her way.

As it turned out, I needed to be cleansed and protected too. I know a lot of people think this kind of stuff is silly, but working with my healer was one of the greatest gifts I've ever given myself, so from my experience I highly recommend it.

We discussed patterns, energy, vibrations, and it all resonated with me on such a deep level. My energy healer put a lot of focus on my self-love tank (it desperately needed to be refueled). She told me that the only way to break the patterns in my life was to *know* that I deserve more. More important, I needed to stop being afraid to *allow* myself more.

Sounds easy? It actually takes a shit-ton of work to put yourself first. I've started to comprehend that if I choose friendships or relationships that are only giving me 50 percent, I'm accepting 50 percent for everything in my life. That means half-assed friendships, half-assed relationships, and a half-assed career. How half-assed is that?

I believe the universe does have a plan for me, and the only thing that shifts that timeline is free will. That's what separates our human self from what the universe has lying in wait for us.

The problem is my human self mostly loves streaming any kind of catching-a-cheater show. That shit gives me *life*.

I'm still trying to find my higher self, but I am not above saging a bitch.

The One, or Not

BEING SINGLE AT THIRTY-SEVEN is as weird as it is wonderful.

When I was younger, I had a plan, and as I went through relationship after relationship I always kept that plan as my end goal. I was going to be married at around thirty-three or thirty-four, with two kids, a house with a rose garden, and a successful career. That was it! The extent of my ambition.

It's crazy how my thoughts have changed as those target years passed me by. Do I still long for a partner? Of course. Thankfully, I'm not jaded. In fact, I'm hopeful. But, I don't spend every waking moment thinking about, waiting for, or planning my future wedding anymore. If it happens, it happens. If it doesn't, it doesn't. And I'm OK with that.

I had to ask myself: Do I still want kids? I think I do. I recently went to the doctor to take a fertility test to make sure my eggs were intact. (They are, and I have time.) Could I do it on my own?

I think I could. Have I considered adoption? I have. Up until this year, my mind had never moved in this direction. The beauty of this changing internal monologue is that it's no longer depressing. It's empowering. I have options. *I can do this all by myself.*

The definition of success, happiness, and fulfillment looks different for everyone. And hey, it should—the times, they are a-changin'. We shouldn't try to achieve a cookie-cutter lifestyle because of what we've seen on TV or in movies, or what we've been told by our parents and society. We shouldn't compare ourselves to other people. It's pointless to envy a life that isn't our own.

The best thing you can do with your life is make your own choices and find the happiness that's right for you. You can be single, or single-ish, or dating, or Actually Dating, or engaged, or married, or divorced, or widowed, and still be fulfilled. Do what's best for you.

I take time to remind myself of my solo successes: I bought a house on my own. I have dogs on my own, even if their dad still comes by to walk them sometimes. I own multiple businesses on my own. Dammit, I can do *anything* on my own! All I had to do was believe in *me.*

These epiphanies didn't come easy, but they have all come to fruition with self-love, something I now make a point to recognize every single day. It takes work. It's a *journey.* But I've accepted that as crazy as my life has been up until now, I've learned a lot. This didn't happen all at once, but one day a lightbulb went off, and I knew, without a doubt, that it was time to put myself first. It was time to love *me.*

At first, I didn't feel like I had the tools to get through things without a crutch, and so I found lots of crutches. Codependency, alcohol, and unhealthy distractions have all been favored coping mechanisms. When I started acknowledging that self-love was my real goal, it made me so anxious. *What if life throws me a curveball, and I'm not able to land on my own two feet?*

I'm learning to shut down that inner voice. Life *will* throw me curveballs, things *are* going to suck sometimes, and not *everything* will go as planned. But isn't that the experience of living? I give myself homework every day, and sometimes I find it silly to hug myself or write down ten things I'm good at. But every little bit helps, and now I finally trust that I *do* love myself. There's nothing more essential in the world. I feel like I'm finally finding a way to own all of my positive attributes and work to shut down negative thoughts. Again, I'm not saying it's easy. But who is more important than yourself?

Be aware of the people you choose to surround yourself with, and how you choose to spend your days. Know that it's OK to say no. It's OK to go to sleep early, and it's OK to sleep alone.

Sometimes I laugh too loud or talk too fast; it's because I'm passionate. Sometimes it's hard for me to take no for an answer, but I get shit done. I laugh at my own jokes before I've told them. I have a reputation that precedes me, but that means I have some pretty killer stories to share. I'm lanky and talk with my hands, kind of like the inflatable balloon man outside of a used car dealership, and you know what? It's because I'm full of excitement. I love my quirks. I stand up for my beliefs—sometimes to the chagrin of others, but I do it anyway. I'm not afraid to dream.

Mostly, I've learned to forgive myself. I know I'm funny. I know I'm kind. I know I'm generous. I know I'm loyal. But most of all, I know I'm crazy. And that's OK.

Please know that *you* are worthy of love and respect. Notice and honor your strengths. Reward yourself for your victories. Don't ever give up on *you*. You're a funny, kind, and crazy chick in the best kind of way.

Writing this book is the most vulnerable thing I've ever done, including being on *Vanderpump Rules*. I'm pretty comfortable in my own skin these days. That doesn't mean I'm perfect, and I still have twinges of self-doubt, but those insecurities are mine to overcome. Trust me when I say this: happy looks SO good on you, better than all the Botox in the world.

How do I promise not to hack into my next boyfriend's email account? Or drive by his place of business and confront his coworker for sending him inappropriate texts? I can't. I'm an open book, and he needs to be the same. The minute my bubble feels a little off, my intuition kicks in. I hope I won't revert to my old ways, because I've done the work, I've taken inventory, and I hold myself responsible.

Sure, I'll still make mistakes, and somebody might even call me "crazy" again—actually, *count* on someone calling me crazy again. Crazy Kristen. But this time I'll own it, and I'll wear it as a badge of honor.

I'm crazy because of all my experiences, all the love and heartbreak, all the happiness and sadness and love and hate. I look back on my life and feel so grateful that I've been lucky enough to have lived so fully, to have met so many wonderful people, and to experience life at its most thrilling every day.

When the time is right and my self-love tank is full, the one will come along. Maybe I know him and maybe I don't.

But at least for now, the one is me.

Acknowledgments

AS I SIT IN MY COZY breakfast nook at home in sunny California penning my gratitude, I'm feeling extremely blessed. When I first went to Michele with an idea, a few pages, and a shitton of dating stories I knew she would be the perfect person to help bring this book to life. Mich, I fucking love you. I never knew a best friendship could grow so quickly, and we literally never get sick of each other. Thinking back on all of the countless hours, early mornings, late nights, and staycations makes me emotional. The process of writing this book with you was one of the most therapeutic and rewarding experiences of my life—you are like a big sister to me. Your experiences, advice, comedic wit, and incredible storytelling ability have made me not only a better writer but a better woman. I can't wait to do this over and over with you, fully caffeinated. Are you ready?

We are so fortunate to have an awesome agent at Fuse Literary, Connor Goldsmith, and editor at Chicago Review Press, Kara Rota. Thank you both for your hunger, dedication, your incredible enthusiasm, and for seeing our vision from the very beginning. "Unpacking" all of my stories and emotions wasn't always the easiest ride but it was so damn worth it. You've loved my crazy from day one.

A massive thank you to our hardworking team at Chicago Review Press! Our publisher Cynthia Sherry, marketing extraordinaire Andrea Baird, PR goddess Alisse Goldsmith-Wissman, cover design shout-out to Jonathan Hahn, interior design genius Sarah Olson, killer managing editor Michelle Williams, production phenom Allison Felus, and to Alex Granato and Alayna Parsons-Valles for mailings, subrights, and generally keeping all of our ducks in a row. All of y'all rock our world.

To *my* rad team, Joe Weiner and Ryan Revel, you handsome devils. I feel like I've known you my entire life so *thank you* for keeping it together. The thousands of phone calls and emails do not go unnoticed. Jennifer Abel, my publicist, you are a damn angel. You not only speak my language but you are just as brilliant at your job as you are at being my friend. You celebrate my psycho but also help my wings grow. I love you.

Shooting the cover for this book was a day I'll never forget. Ian Maddox, I couldn't have imagined anyone else bringing the cover photo to life but you. I am awkward and typically hate photos of myself, yet somehow you so effortlessly ignite the spark in me. To my glam fam Jared Lipscomb, Bradley Leake, and Anais Cordova: glam fams aren't just artists, thank you for being mini therapists and always making me look like I have my shit together even when I don't. Georgia Mitropoulos, you are such a baller stylist. You get my vibe and made our cover shoot so killer. After working on my very first photo shoot, it was pure magic to get to do this again together over fifteen years later. Detroit, baby!

Lisa Vanderpump (and Ken Todd), thank you for giving me a leg up on business and branding, for the tough love (yes, I mean that), and giving me the opportunity of a lifetime on *Vanderpump Rules*. To everyone at Bravo and NBCU, specifically Andy Cohen, Frances Berwick, Jennifer Geisser, Shari Levine, Ryan Flynn, Sheonna Mix, Chloe Bremner, and Paige DuBois—I can never express the gratitude I hold. I would have never been given the platform to write my stories in a book if it weren't for all of you and our show.

Evolution Media, you are my framily. First and foremost, the creators of *Vanderpump Rules*—Alex Baskin and Douglas Ross—for taking a chance on a bunch of twenty-something-year-old waiters and seeing the potential we had to make some crazy, sexy, and cool television. Thank you to my showrunner, Bill Langworthy, for being the number one man in my life to deal with, wrangle, and somehow put Crazy Kristen on a pedestal for so many years. John Carr, Jeremiah Smith, Jenna Rosenfeld, Erin Foye, Lyndsay Burr, Sun DeGraaf, Mikayla Ferrin, *all* of my field producers (past and present), and to every single human on the *Vanderpump Rules* production crew: You ALL are the unsung heroes—watching me cry, scream, fall, laugh, and grow over the past eight years. You get that relationships are hard.

My O.G. *Vanderpump Rules* cast: Peter Madrigal, Katie Maloney, Tom Sandoval, Stassi Schroeder, Tom Schwartz, Scheana Shay, Jax Taylor—I sincerely love each and every one of you. What we've been through together no one will ever understand or comprehend. You know many of these stories firsthand, and we have a bond that I will cherish forever.

Brittany Cartwright, thank you for being everything you are: patient, humble, and kind. You truly are the epitome of what a best friend looks like and you never *once* made me feel crazy.

To my girl Ariana Madix, you are such a huge part of my story. Thank you for giving this crazy girl a chance and for our unlikely friendship coming out on top. You taught me to respond rather than react and I'd like to think I taught you it's okay to just LIVE, LAUGH, and LOVE.

And to Lala Kent, you've always been an honest straight shooter with me. You're one of kind, bitch. Keep *giving them Lala.*

Writing this book was so nostalgic and at times really made me miss my home back in Michigan. I am incredibly lucky to have some amazing L.A. friends I call family. When you date as many guys as I have you need your tribe, and when you find your tribe, love them hard. Rachael Nicole O'Brien, you gorgeous creature of a woman. We will never break the chain. You are an incredible workhorse, and thank you for introducing me to my book agent. You knew I had to expel these stories! You have taught me so much, constantly pushing me to be a better writer and allowing me to ride your comedy coattails. Zack Wickham, you are my sounding board and my support system. Honestly, thanks for keeping my damn life together, whether it's packing a suitcase or unpacking my feelings. David Grant, I don't know if this book would have been possible without you. It was your idea for Michele and I to pair up, so essentially I am awarding the most credit to your handsome self. James Kirtley, thank you for your support and stories and for giving us your Palm Springs writing retreat home. You are an amazing friend; we love you. Erin Waddell, our cult bond and friendship will last a lifetime. Kirstin MacMillan, I am so grateful to have you in my life for taking care of my puppy sons. Alex Menache, you big idiot full of knowledge, kindness, affection, and grace—those forty roses will always count. Cassia Hoffman, Jeanine Carter, Courtney Berman, Jayme Foxx, Jo Wenberg, Magen Mattox, and mostly my hometown ride-or-dies Amy Anderson, Jeff Vella, Rachelle Rotunda, and Phil Delaney—you've lived these stories with me and walked me through some of the hardest times.

Shout out to my self-care team: Val, Serah, Heather, and Angie! REAL SELF LOVE, BABY! That's what it's all about.

Most important, to my incredible family back home in Detroit: Mom, you birthed me. I literally owe you the world. Grandma Doute, RyRy, Sav, and Jess, you are the rocks that keep me grounded. Doutes don't give up, we persevere. To my sissy, Casey Zacker, thank you for being the best big sister, hands down the funniest person I know, and for your incredible artistic nature. Thank God I remembered you could draw! I couldn't think of anyone more perfect to illustrate my dating life in a book. *I wrote a book and you illustrated it!* No one gets me better than you do.

Carter, you will always be one of my best friends and my puppy-baby-daddy forever and a day.

Annnnd . . . last but definitely not least: hats off to the rest of the guys who made me crazy.

John, Johnny, Joey, Danny, Joe, Thom, Eric, Scott, Chris, Christopher, Sean, Matt, Garri, Mark, Mike, Blake, Max, Craig, Nick, Andy, Jeff, Jimmy, and Ian.

Without you all, I wouldn't be the strong butterfly I am today.